Golf Vacations In California

A Complete Guide to
All Golf Resorts in California

Eliane Pepper
Pinehurst Publishing, Inc.

Golf Vacations in California

A complete guide to all resorts in California

by Eliane Pepper

Published by:

Pinehurst Publishing, Inc.
P.O.Box 3144
Manhattan Beach, CA. 90266
(213)545-3318
FAX (213)545-8971

Editor: Elaine Osio
Cover design by Robert Howard
Resort drawings and maps by Chuck Osborn
Book design by Pauline Howard
Meadowood drawing by Earl Thollander

Pepper, Eliane,
Golf Vacations in California/by Eliane Pepper
LC#90-091563
ISBN 0-9625778-0-1
Golf vacations/resorts California, USA.

Printed in Singapore

Softcover: $14.95

Disclaimer

This book is designed to provide information on golf resorts and golf courses plus the areas where they are located. It is sold with the understanding that the publisher and author are not engaged in the travel business. If a travel agent's services are required, then the services of a competent professional should be sought.

This book does not provide all the information available about each resort and geographical area described in each chapter.

Every effort has been made to make the information given in this book as accurate as possible. However there may be occasional mistakes. Resort prices, for instance, vary continuously. Therefore, this book should be used as a guide only. Specific information should be acquired at the time the trip is scheduled and reservations are made with the respective resorts and courses. Furthermore, this book contains only information available to us up to the time of printing.

The author and Pinehurst Publishing, Inc. shall have neither liability nor responsibility to any person(s)or business group(s)with respect to any loss or damage caused or alleged to have been caused directly or indirectly by the information provided in this book.

If you do not agree with the above, you may return this book to the publisher for a full refund.

Table of Contents

The "notable" public golf course in Northern California:

Resorts in Central California:

The "notable" public courses in Central California:

Resorts in Southern California:

The "notable" golf courses in Southern California:

A note to the reader

I wrote this book with the intent of guiding and informing the reader. I've drawn from my own experience at these resorts and golf courses, and eventually developed the criteria for the listing of the resorts in this book.

Resorts must guarantee specific starting times over the phone, rather than have a "loose" arrangement with public or private courses in the area, which means that sometimes they can get starting times, but not always....

Sometimes a golf course flanked by condominiums will call itself a golf resort, but it does not have the proper hotel services and accommodations. It simply rents out these condos for seasonal use by the weekend, week, or month. Most of the time the condos, casitas or whatever one wishes to call them are privately owned. This means that you would be staying in someone's home, using their linen, plates, silverware and taking your chances on the interior design and guest comforts. I cannot accept these as "resorts," and I am not listing them.

I happen to have a low tolerance level for poor food service and sagging beds. But, allowing for the fact that we don't all like the same things, I have done my best to be as fair as possible in the coverage of each golf resort, with minimum bias. Sometimes I try to warn the reader through omission rather than to be totally negative. Fortunately, most of my research has been rewarding. I think that says a lot for the standards of quality of the golf resorts in California.

I am sure that you'll have fun. And I hope you'll let me know how this book helped you on your vacation.

When you return home after after your 7 and/or 10 day golf vacation, I would very much like to hear from you... tell me:

Did my suggestions help you to play as much golf as possible?

Did you find the resorts' descriptions accurate?

Should any changes be made regarding the resort's descriptions and statistics?

Did you discover any interesting places off the beat-and-path you would care to share with the other readers?

If you care to share your discoveries or comments, please mail them to me at: P.O.Box 3144, Manhattan Beach, CA. 90266

Thank you,

Eliane Pepper

CHAPTER I

Fore-Play....

Fore-Play...

In this chapter, I share with my readers golf travel tips learned from experience growing out of diverse, but always fun-filled trips.

Pre-plan your trip and eliminate frustration and wasted time during your priceless vacation.

Ask questions, lots of questions, when making your reservations... and always use the (800) number. Most resorts offer this convenience for reservation purposes. This book lists them all.

While on the phone, ask about:

.... *Golf Packages:* Find out if your resort offers a "golf package." If so, take advantage of it; most packages can save you a lot of money compared to the same amenities offered a-la-carte. "Package" questions to ask: Seasonal prices and their cut off dates? How much for additional nights? Do they include unlimited golf, electric golf carts, tennis, driving range balls, bag, and shoe storage? Are breakfast and dinner included?

Regarding dinner... there was a time when hotel restaurants were a stop of last resort. Today, most resorts hire the great chefs away from prestigious restaurants; therefore, not only do the resort guests enjoy their culinary expertise but these restaurants are also coveted by the locals. It is therefore necessary to make your dinner reservations while booking your vacation, at least for the night of your arrival.

If writing each resort for up-to-date information is a time consuming bother, then use one of the mail/FAX order coupons in the back of this book, and we will mail back to you the actual brochures of all the resorts listed in this book. When available, even copies of their menus.

Alcoholic beverages are always an extra item and so are taxes. A few resorts will automatically add an additional 15% to your bill for gratuities;

ask... or you may find yourself tipping cash for services only to find out too late that you'll be tipping twice as you glare at your bill.

Even if your resort does not offer a golf package, don't forget to ask if gratuities are automatically added to your bill.

.... ***Starting times:*** How would you like to arrive at a golf resort, check in, ask for a starting time on the first day and be turned down because there aren't any times available? It happens. Remember, if you're a golfer, you're in a golf resort to play golf... and so is just about everyone else. Starting times can be snapped up at the speed of light. To avoid disappointment, keep in mind that your golf starting times will not automatically be set up for you by the reservation clerk, even if you're reserving a "golf package." You do that yourself by requesting and, if need be, insisting, that your starting times be given to you right then and there, and that the time given to you over the phone be confirmed in writting, time permitting. It's a good idea to tell the reservation clerck the approximate range of starting times preferable to you for each day of your stay.

Of course you don't want to go to a resort that can't accommodate your vacation objective: golf and more golf...

.... ***Phone calls from your room:*** Find out the resort's policy regarding phone charges. Charging guests a phone call fee each time they either make a direct call or use their credit card has became another profit center for many hotels. If you think that this concern is petty, then you haven't been presented with these charges that can amount to $1.00 or more per call. It is even worse if their long distance phone company is not the same as the one shown on your credit card.

.... ***Eating out?*** Most resort areas boast excellent restaurants or eateries to please most palates. But if you want to search the area for restaurants, then I suggest that you start your research before leaving home. Get a copy of books written by food critics with knowledge of the restaurants in the area. You'll find suggestions worth exploring during your vacation, but only after golf...

.... ***The Concierge Connection:*** The hotel guest's best friend, not to be confused with the Bell Captain....

The Concierge is well-informed and an expert on the city, and can arrange everything from theatre tickets to change of airline reservations, unexpected doctor's appointments to spur-of-the moment weddings.

It is customary to tip the concierge for information or services performed. Much too often, the bell captain or bellman who delivers the airline ticket or the flowers for your Valentine is the one who gets the tip, but all he's done is deliver the item. He didn't spend his time on the phone "making it happen."

.... ***To find out what's going on...*** plays, movies, museum exhibits, local celebrations, sports events; etc... buy the area's magazine; ask for the issue covering that month's events. This service can be provided by the Concierge at your chosen resort. But please, mail a check for his/her services and magazines costs. The local Sunday paper is also a fruitful source of information. And most important, go to your local Auto Club and get a map of California plus another map for your specific destination. Getting lost is not something to file under "memory lane."

.... ***Resort clothes are not dress-up clothes.*** Simplify your life and have fun... You'll dress for golf in the morning and stay that way all day long, unless you play tennis, go swimming or horseback riding. The only other change you'll need is for dinner. Even if it's dinner and dance, or dinner and theatre, the fashionable man or woman is in "resort casual" attire.

> My boy friend and I once traveled with another couple who brought a suitcase full of evening dresses, dark suits, shirts and ties. At dinner, he looked like he was going to a business lunch in downtown Tokyo and she looked like the Queen of the Stardust Ballroom!

One suitcase for each person is really all you'll need, regardless of how long you are vacationing in California. Resorts will take care of your cleaning and laundry. No time for laundry while resort hopping? Yes, there is. Send your clothes to be cleaned as soon as you check in (wait until you get to your room), and tell the service person when you'd like the clothes back in your closet. This system beats repacking and unpacking dirty clothes.

Your golf bag cover is a great place to pack your golf sweaters, windbreakers, corduroy pants, socks, many golf balls (throw away the boxes), and shoes. It's a good idea to put the golf shoes inside a lined shoe bag to prevent the spikes from cutting either your golf bag or the golf bag cover. This method of packing also cushions and protects your golf clubs from the airline's raging-maniacal baggage handlers.

.... ***Baby-sitters:*** Your best bet is calling the hotel concierge to find out if this service is available, and how far in advance you need to give notice to reserve the sitter's time. But, most important... you'll want to know how the hotel is responsible for the sitter. Who is the baby-sitter? Get references from other guests (you must check out guests' names and get their phone numbers from the hotel's registration records). You, and only you, must make this phone call, and then follow up with a call to the prospective sitter. You must rely on your instincts just as much as on the information given to you... you can't be too careful or ask too many questions, conserning this item...

.... ***Rent-a-car or a van?*** For three or more people, always a van... Clubs and suitcases just don't fit into most trunks. Personally, I don't care to cuddle up to my golf bag in the back seat... and, don't forget to inquire when making your reservation, if you'll be able to leave the vehicle at a location other than the pick-up area. This may or may not be apropos. But if it is, check carefully or you may be paying an unexpected premium.

.... ***Boarding your pet:*** Information can be obtained from the concierge. You might be able to take the pet to the resort's door and have (by prearranged reservation) the pet boarding house pick up your pet from you.

.... ***In conclusion,*** preparing and pre-planning your vacation will prevent headaches and frustration during your well-deserved time-of-your life. And the additional bonus.... the more you plan and research your trip, the more you'll be living your vacation before leaving home. Isn't that exciting?

CHAPTER II

Is there life after golf?

Life after golf...The Monterey Peninsula

This is a photographer's paradise... one of the most beautiful areas in California, offering the vacationer magnificent coastal and forest environments, historical sites, Victorian architecture, and post-card perfect villages.

The 17-Mile Drive is a must, with many scenic points of interest. Since all the resorts and golf courses are located within, you'll have plenty of opportunities to explore its beautiful sites.

For a change of pace, how about a trip to the world renowned Monterey Aquarium. One of the unusual attractions is the above-and-below water tank for observing the endangered sea otters.

Monterey was Spanish California's first capital. Several of its historical buildings have been preserved in the Path of History, which is well marked for self-guided tours.

John Steinbeck once made Cannery Row famous. Now, it houses several upscale restaurants, hotels, antique shops, and art galleries. The First Theatre, on Scott St., is definitely a "don't miss".

Pacific Grove, west of Monterey, is the home of the famous Butterfly Trees. Every winter, thousands of brightly colored orange and black butterflies migrate to a six-acre grove of trees. The Butterfly Parade draws spectators to town every October. Pacific Grove is known too, for its Feast of Lanterns in July and its Victorian House Tour in April. Just walking around town you'll spot several of the Victorians.

The village of Carmel is a quaint place to shop or just walk, and people watch. One of my favorite places is the Tuck House, for afternoon tea served with homemade scones.

Carmel has long been a mecca for artists and writers. Robinson Jeffers was known as the poet laureate of the Monterey Coast. You may wish to tour his home, The Tor House, built in 1919, on a cliff overlooking Carmel Bay. The house is shown by reservation only.

Big Sur is a spectacular, winding scenic drive along the coast, not to be driven in a hurry. Don't even think of rushing through Big Sur. The way to enjoy it is to drive south (down the coast), so that you can enjoy the ocean scenery on your right. Plan for a four-hour drive to San Simeon. You'll cross at least 27 bridges in a stretch of 75 miles. The Bixby bridge spans 330 feet, crossing a gorge 200 feet below. It's the longest concrete-arch span in the world. You can walk on it, enjoy the ocean view, and don't forget the camera....

Climate: Summer, average temperature is 67°
Winter, average temperature is 57°

In summer you can expect cool, foggy mornings and warm afternoons. Fall is the sunny season: it lasts from August through December. In the Carmel Valley you can count on very hot days and warm nights in the summer months. You'll be wise to pack a raincoat.

Life after golf... The Napa Valley

To most people Napa Valley is synonymous with "The Wine Country," and with good reason. More than 60 wineries are spaced at close intervals between Yountville and Calistoga, surrounded by more than 26,000 acres of grapevines covering the valley floor.

A leisurely trip to a few wineries after golf is a pleasant way to begin your "life after golf". But please don't hurry from winery to winery like some crazed tourist who thinks the valley is going to run out of wine... To really appreciate the wineries and wine tasting, I suggest no more than two wineries a day. Each winery has its own style of architecture and different lessons to be learned on wine-making and tasting. To cite two: Domaine Chandon dared to be the first and so far the only winery to be of modern design. Barrel-vault ceilings cover a stone, concrete and glass-walled building. At Chandon you'll be introduced to the fermented-in-the-bottle method of brewing sparkling wines. Second, while at Beaulieu Vineyard you will listen to one of the most descriptive narrations of the state of international winemaking in modern times. The oldest of the buildings dates back to 1885, and touring the buildings will require a sober sense of direction.

Free folders listing wineries in the region are available from the Wine Institute, 165 Post St., San Francisco, CA. 94108.

Napa Valley has a number of very good restaurants, but few enough that reservations are required.

On another level, Napa's hills offer the right kind of air to glider pilots who take off and land at the little airport in Calistoga. Balloon flights over the valley, where you'll have a birds-eye view of the wineries and vineyards, can be arranged by the Concierge at your resort.

Ever seen a pig rolling around in the mud? I never have, but that's what I thought of when I saw the famous mud-baths in Calistoga. Now that I've expressed my opinion, I'll add that a lot of people love mud.... Then there is the Geyser... it's rather interesting, you wait 35 or 40 minutes while it gurgles, burps and belches, and then it finally gushes forth.... Frankly, I would rather play another 9-holes....

Climate: The weather relatively mild, except in the summer months which are around 100°. Winters have sporadic rain, very seldom sleet or snow.

Life after Golf... The Central Coast

From Morro Bay down to Oxnard is what we call the Central Coast.

Trivia.... The second largest monolith in the world is in Morro Bay. The 576-foot-high Morro Rock stands in the bay, connected to shore by a thin strip of land.

Morro Bay is a fishing village. And as in most fishing villages, the fresh fish served in its restaurants is very good, even if the restaurants are very casual and without a trace of elegance.

San Luis Obispo is the half-way point between Los Angeles and San Francisco. The Mission, founded in 1772, still stands today. A tour of San Luis Obispo is not complete without a tour of the Madonna Inn, a hotel with two hundred fantasy/nightmare designed rooms. I am of the opinion that somebody had a very bad architectural dream, and why they ever wanted to perpetuate it by building such a monstrosity is beyond me. You've got to see it to believe it!

If you like to browse at art fairs, Santa Barbara is the place. Every Sunday an arts-and-crafts show is held along Cabrillo Blvd. The city also has a packed annual program catering to all tastes and interests, the high-light being the Old Spanish Days fiesta from the first days of July to August 3. The Summer Music Festival is held at the Lobera Theater and the incredible Concours d'Elegance antique car parade is held in September. October is highlighted by the week-long arts festival.

A short drive from Santa Barbara is the San Marcos Pass, where palomino parade horses are methodically bred. On a clear day, you'll see the Channel Islands Chain and the Santa Inez Valley.

The Santa Barbara Chamber of Commerce has provided convenient visitors' signposts: one set designed for the "on foot" tourists, and another for the "by car" group that takes you to the stately Spanish-Moorish county

Court House, one of the most beautiful public buildings in the USA, the Santa Barbara Museum of Art, the Carriage Museum, and the El Paseo arcade, for bargain hunters.

Last, but definitely worth doing, is a drive through Montecito, to catch a glimpse of the wealthy estates. Stopping in the village for an afternoon cappuccino in one of their small cafés or a drink at the lovely old San Ysidro Guest Ranch.

Climate: The coastal average temperature in the summer is 75°, in the winter is 60°. The Ojai and Solvang valleys are hot in the summer months, with tempeatures rising to 100°.

Life after golf?.... The Desert Area

The Desert area of Southern California where golf resorts are located includes Palm Springs, Palm Desert, Rancho Mirage, Cathedral City, Indian Wells and La Quinta.

With a total of 80 golf courses in the Desert, it's amazing that one can still see a desert landscape when looking up at the surrounding mountains. Floating over Palm Springs in a hot-air balloon, one sees more green and lush fairways than desert sand.

Write for an issue of the magazine *Palm Springs Life* while planning your trip. This magazine has a *Desert Guide* supplement in every issue that will give you up-to-date information from entertainment to nature walks and museum listings. Also worthwhile for the golfer is an issue of *Golf News* magazine with all the chitchat about the local Desert golf life. This magazine lists the up-coming Celebrity and Pro Tournaments. It's fun to visit the resorts where these tournaments are played and mingle with the "celebrities." You'll see lots of them coming and going in the public areas of the hotels.

Aside from what the resorts have to offer during the day and evening, there is always shopping... the El Paseo strip in Palm Desert has many of the renowned shops of Beverly Hills' Rodeo Drive plus other local specialty shops.

Hot air balloon rides can be a photographer's paradise. There are flights at sunrise and sunset daily from October through April.

The Living Desert offers a close-up view of animals and plants, and frequent week end programs of Indian dancing. Most of the land in Palm Springs is leased from the Indians. No wonder they're dancing....

The McCallum Theatre has different performances of jazz and pop music, plus symphonies and light opera.

One should not miss a trip up the Aerial Tramway, 8500 ft. to the top of the San Jacinto Mountain, where cross-country skiers pursue excellent trails in winter, and walkers and hikers can enjoy them in summer. If you do neither one, you'll still delight in the breathtaking view of the Desert. Imagine... playing golf while your non-golfing family or friends cross-country ski on the same day.... Only in Southern California.

... Assorted activities:

The Palm Desert Town Center has an ice-skating rink. The El Dorado Polo Club invites guests to picnic while enjoying the matches.

Truly memorable horseback riding in some of the Desert's most spectacular scenery is offered by the Ranch of the Seventh Range.

The former Roy Rogers/Gene Autry Movie Ranch near Yucca Valley has old-fashioned country entertainment every week.

You have to eat ... so explore the restaurant scene. Read a good restaurant guidebook before leaving home. Gourmets have researched the area thoroughly.

... Golf Trivia:

There are more golf courses here than in any other resort area in California. The courses are open year round. But the summer months are quite hot and golf is usually played in the very early morning or after 4:00 PM.

In Palm Springs, unlike other California golf resort areas, one can get starting times with relative ease at most courses open to the public. By that I mean one does not have to start dialing the phone at dawn, only to hear the unfriendly sound of a busy signal for at least thirty minutes before getting through to the starter. Then, if you are lucky, a starting time is yours...seven days away. In the desert, a call one or two days in advance is usually enough. Depending on the day of the week and season, one can even get starting times at resorts that allow public play.

The preferable time to vacation in Palm Springs is from October through May. However, the first two weeks of June still allow one to enjoy the game all day and take advantage of the reduced summer rates that begin after May 31.

The fairways in the resort courses are always quite lush, and the greens are superbly manicured except during seeding time (October and early November).

Climate:

October/April:	Days 70/75°	Nights: 26/50°
May/June:	Days 85/95°	Nights: 50/70°
July/September:	Days 105/115°	Nights: 80/90°

Life after golf....San Diego and Vicinity

San Diego has a lot to offer the golfer's family. The subject is really a book all by itself. The following suggestions represent a fraction of the extensive menu of activities available for your pleasure in San Diego.

In Old Town, you'll find the best Mexican food north of the border as well as a very good collection of shops merchandising Mexican art, clothes, jewelry and home accessories. Also, don't neglect visiting Horton Plaza, across from the Grant Hotel downtown, which houses the best shops and department stores in San Diego and several movie theatres.

The San Diego Civic Theater and Symphony and Opera House are all within easy reach.

La Jolla, derived from the Spanish word "jewel," is truly a jewel in a magnificent setting. World travelers have acclaimed its beautiful beaches, lovely hotels, and gourmet restaurants. Connoisseurs of art, music and drama can indulge their interests by visiting the many private galleries and the La Jolla Museum of Contemporary Art.

Sea World of San Diego has for the past 20 years been graded number two family attraction in California, second only to Disneyland. There are several exciting shows, such as the "Shamu Celebration," where trainer and killer whale interact to exhibit the close relationship between man and sea mammal.

There are over 3200 animals living in the San Diego Zoo, which is also a Botanical Garden filled with exotic plants and colorful flowers.

In Balboa Park you may want to visit the Museum of Man, Natural History Museum, San Diego Museum of Art, Aero Space Museum and the Reuben H. Fleet Space Theatre and Science Center. The Old Globe Theatre, presents Shakespearian performances second to none, every summer.

The San Diego Harbor has an impressive collection of our great World War II battleships in mothballs that can be viewed while sailing or motor-boating around the harbor. There are several harbor excursions aboard schooners offering cocktails, dinner and dancing.

Temecula Valley Wine Country was first discovered in the 1840's by Jean Louis Vignes, and re-discovered in the 1960's by the local growers. Since then, award-winning wines from the Temecula Valley have been served to connoisseurs all over the world. Callaway, Hart, Piconi and Culbertson Wineries are within minutes of one another and worth a "wine tasting" visit. You can easily spend an afternoon browsing through the many antique shops in the Old Town of Temecula.

Bonsall is the home of the famous San Luis Rey Downs' stables. The Training center is one of the world's finest and largest facilities for Triple Crown hopefuls. You may want to schedule an appointment to view the thoroughbreds in training at the Center.

You should contact the *San Diego Tourist Bureau* or your local *Automobile Club* for information on San Diego plus an up-to-date map of the entire San Diego area.

The climate is mild year-around.

CHAPTER III

Golf.... everyday!

Golf... 7-days in Northern California

Let's start this vacation in Napa Valley. Your choice of Resorts... Silverado or Meadowood... are both excellent. However as a guest at Silverado, you'll be able to play their two courses, and still have access to the Chardonay golf course.

Day 1 - You have arrived at the Silverado Resort, and will now check in at the pro-shop for your starting time mid-day at one of the courses, North or South. I hate to see people slowing down play on a golf course to take pictures; but, let's make an exception and carry a camera if you're playing the South Course, just in case you should be lucky enough to see the family of deer around one of the greens. Dinner at The Oak, requiring only resort-casual attire, may be just the right place after traveling and 18-holes. If you still have any energy left, dance the night away on the veranda after dinner; if not, there's always tomorrow night.

Day 2 - You now have time for an early round on the North course. Enjoy lunch in St. Helene, just 10 minutes away, and then visit a couple of vineyards. You'll be back at the resort in time to change for dinner... perhaps you'll drive to Meadowood for cocktails and dinner giving you the opportunity to see this lovely resort.

Day 3 - Where do you want to play today? A repeat of one of the Silverado's courses or how about conquering the Chardonay course? Whatever it is, do it early, because you have a four hour drive to the Monterey Peninsula, where you should check in at either The Lodge in Pebble Beach or the Inn at Spanish Bay in time for dinner.

Day 4 - A mid-morning round at Pebble Beach would still give you time to drive the 17-Mile Drive on the way to Carmel for a walk in the late afternoon, stopping for tea and scones before deciding where you're going to have dinner.

Day 5 - For a totally different golfing experience, you might want to play Spanish Bay or the also challenging Spyglass early morning, so that you'll have time to visit Monterey and one of its many attractions listed in the "There's Life After Golf" chapter. Dinner at one of the Monterey restaurants is a must.

Day 6 - Today, after checking out of your resort, it's a short drive to Carmel Valley to check into either the Carmel Valley Ranch or the Quail's Lodge and play the resort's golf course. How about just relaxing, or maybe taking another trip to either Carmel, Monterey or to discover Pacific Grove's panoramic sights?

Day 7 - This is the last day of your vacation. There's time for a round of golf at either Carmel Valley Resort before heading to Monterey Airport, where you'll drop off your rental car and fly away, or drive on home.

Note: On this 7-day vacation, unlike the other 7-and-10-day-vacations, I have not started the vacation on any particular day of the week. Because resorts in this area seem to offer the same "golf-packages" weekdays or weekends.

Golf... 7-days in Central California

Golfing and sightseeing up the coast from Los Angeles to Central California is a relaxing, laidback way to spend 7 days.

We'll make a couple of assumptions.... First, that your vacation starts on a Saturday, and second, that Los Angeles is the point of departure.

Saturday: Industry Hills Sheraton Resort is the beginning of your "golf junket". Either "The Ike" or "The Babe" courses could be played today. In the evening, there's always Disneyland, the theatres, the symphony, the opera, hockey, and great restaurants. It's impossible to list everything to do in Los Angeles. The *L.A.Times*, Sunday edition, available on Saturdays, is an excellent guide to L.A.

Sunday: Morning starting times at either of the "Industry" courses will be after 10:AM... Then, time to leave L.A. and head north to the Ojai Valley Inn. Plan to arrive there in time for a romantic dinner at the Inn. Because you've arranged for the Sunday through Thursday "golf package", dinner is included.

Monday: After breakfast, 18 holes of golf.... Lunch on the veranda, overlooking the golf course, is a must before riding a bike to the village of Ojai for some antique browsing .

Tuesday: Drive on to the Santa Inez Valley, and check in at the Alisal Guest Ranch, then play 18-holes. There should be time left over to visit the Danish town of Solvang in the afternoon. Why not treat yourself to a Danish Pastry in one of the pastry shops, relax, and watch the tourist world around you? Dinner at the Ranch will be casual and hearty. After all, don't we travel on our stomachs?

Wednesday: La Purissima is only 10 miles away; it's one of the public golf courses definitely worth playing. Ask the Pro at Alisal to arrange for a starting time for you in the early morning, so that you are finished playing before the wind comes up around 1:00 PM. You'll then have the entire afternoon to drive over to Los Olivos and visit a winery or two in the Santa Inez Valley. Los Olivos has lots of good art galleries. The Grand Hotel offers high tea every afternoon.

Thursday: Well, you only have a 7-day vacation.... So, on to Black Lake for another 18 holes. Because there is absolutely nothing to do there after golf, drive to San Luis Obispo for a night's stay at one of the area's Bed and Breakfasts and dinner at one of the good restaurants there. Or, instead of stopping in San Luis Obispo, continue on to Morro Bay, an additional 20 miles, to the Hyatt Hotel overlooking the bay and the "Rock". Sea food abounds at several very casual but good restaurants in the village.

Friday: Morro Bay is known for its foggy mornings, so try for a starting time after 9:00 AM. Your bags are packed...and after golf, it is now time to start driving back to LA. You are either going straight back to the airport for a night-flight home or you can still enjoy another day of golf on Saturday. If so, stop at the Biltmore Four Seasons in Santa Barbara for the night.

Saturday: A starting time at Sandpiper is not easy to get...the Biltmore, given enough notice, can reserve one for you.

Driving notes: You can drive North to Ojai either on the coast route (hwy 1) or via the San Fernando Valley (I-101). The coast highway offers a panoramic view of the Pacific and a peek at Malibu. It's only 4 miles longer than going through the Valley. Well worth it! But not in the summer months when traffic is bumper-to-bumper....

Golf... 10-days in Southern California

Ten days is the ideal length for a relaxed trip...

Let's assume that you'll start your vacation on a weekend... Friday?

Friday: If you arrive in San Diego in the morning you can drive to Singing Hills, where you'll stay 2 nights. Play a round of golf at either the Willow Glen or the Oak Glen courses. Dinner at the resort's restaurant would be the logical thing to do tonight.

Saturday: Play 18-holes in the morning as early as possible and, after finishing, drive to San Diego. Lots to do there....there are the Zoo, Sea World, beaches, shopping at the Horton Plaza (downtown San Diego); if this last is your choice, be sure to stop either for a late lunch or for dinner at the Grant Grill at the Grant Hotel, across the street from the Plaza. Although I don't usually recommend restaurants because I think that there are plenty of responsible professionals who research restaurants on a full-time basis, I really have to tell you about their "mock turtle" soup... fabulous! You might also want to catch a movie at one of the Horton Plaza movie houses.

Sunday: Leave Singing Hills and stop at the San Vicente Country Club for 18-holes (you would, of course, have made reservations ahead of time, or have asked the Singing Hills pro to give you the courtesy of arranging the starting times). After golf, drive on to Rancho Bernardo, where you'll take advantage of their golf package, which includes breakfasts and dinners. Hopefully, you'll arrive in time for high tea. Check in, relax, and get ready to enjoy a gourmet dinner at the El Bizcocho restaurant.

Monday: Play 18-holes at the RB course. Still feel like more golf? Go over to the executive course, just 5 minutes from the resort and also included in your golf package. If not, relax, and enjoy the resort's other amenities. Dinner is still included...

Tuesday: Breakfast, and either play RB again (in the package) or check out and drive on to Pala Mesa for a round of golf. After a nice lunch, drive north to Temecula for dinner and plan to spend the night there, taking advantage of your new golf package.

Wednesday: Golf at Temecula Creek, then time off to visit the wineries and antique shops in the Old Town of Temecula. I suggest dinner again at TCI. Ask the Pro to help you get starting times for tomorrow's golf at the Rancho California Public Course.

Thursday: Relax after golf at one of Temecula Creek's courses, or explore more sights or have lunch at the Culbertson winery overlooking the vineyards. Drive on to the Inn at Rancho Santa Fe for the night, and enjoy a delicious gourmet dinner at the Inn.

Friday: More golf... If your muscles are not begging for a day off, play the private golf course, Rancho Santa Fe Country Club, then look over the village, which is really very quaint, and enjoy another dinner at the Inn. Or maybe you'll discover another great restaurant while strolling in the village.

Saturday: Now let's drive on to La Costa, the totally self contained resort where one can golf or simply take advantage of their extensive spa facilities, wonderful spa cuisine, or more caloric intake at one of their elegant restaurants. In the evening, there is always a movie, dancing or just a quiet rest....

Sunday: Time to go home ... before or after another round of golf. After all, this is a golf purist's vacation. Of course, a real golf massochist may want to get 36 holes in every day, during daylight savings time that is certainly a mad possibility.

CHAPTER IV

Maps

Monterey Peninsula and the Carmel Valley Resorts and Public Course

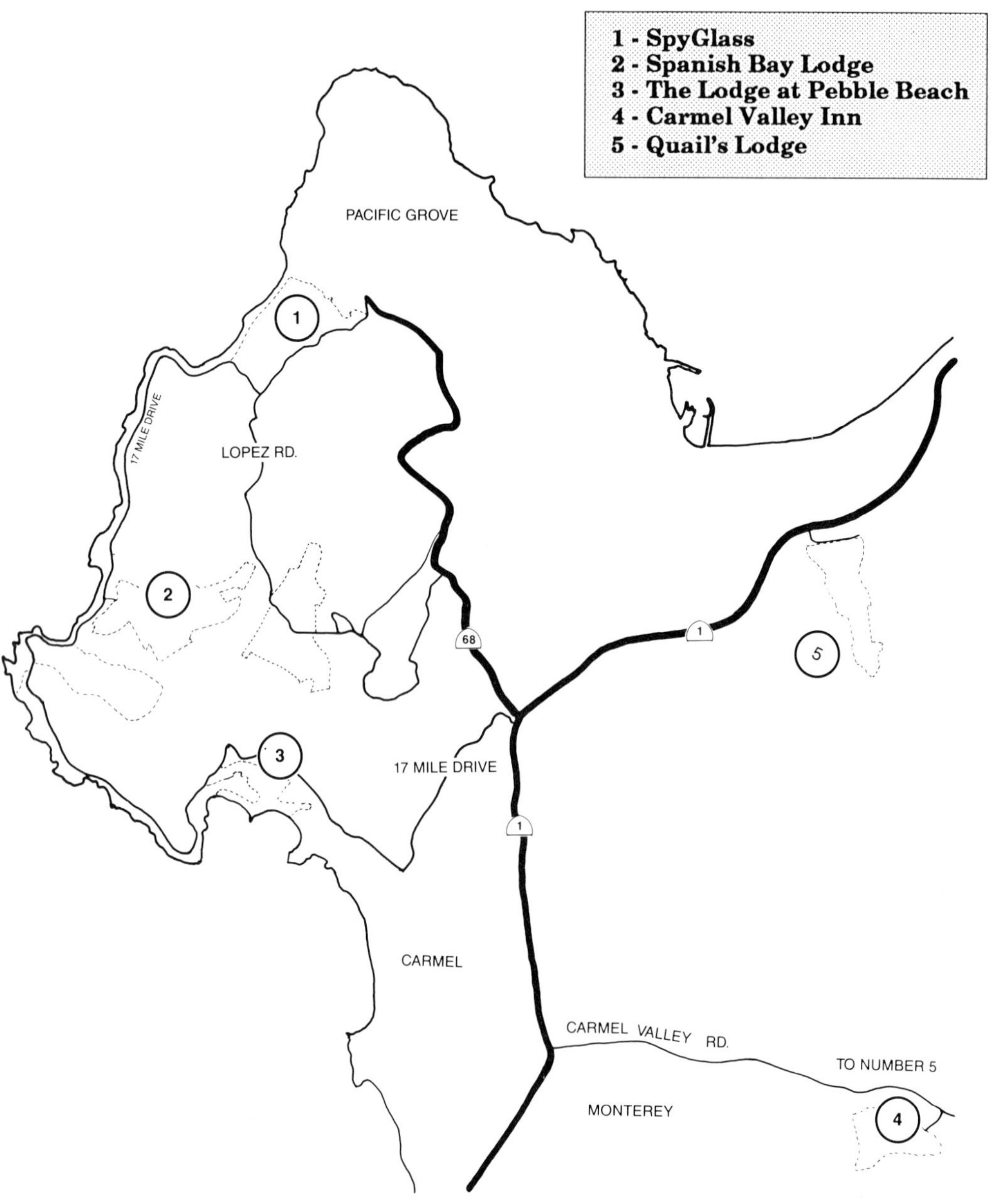

Resorts in Northern California

1 - Meadowood Resort
2 - Silverado Resort
3 - Rancho Murieta Lodge

Map of Resorts and Public Golf Courses in the Central Coast

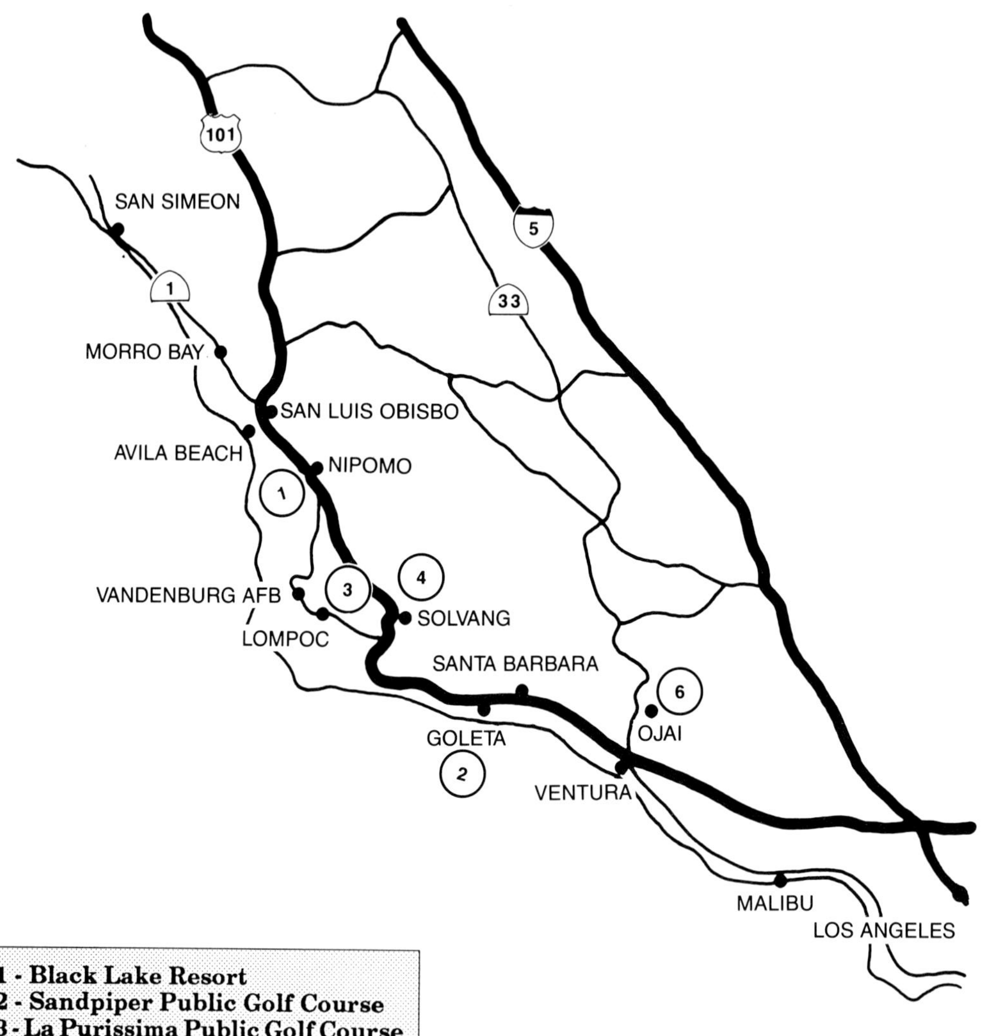

1 - Black Lake Resort
2 - Sandpiper Public Golf Course
3 - La Purissima Public Golf Course
4 - The Alisal Guest Ranch
6 - Ojai Inn

Resorts and Public Golf Courses in the San Diego area and vicinity

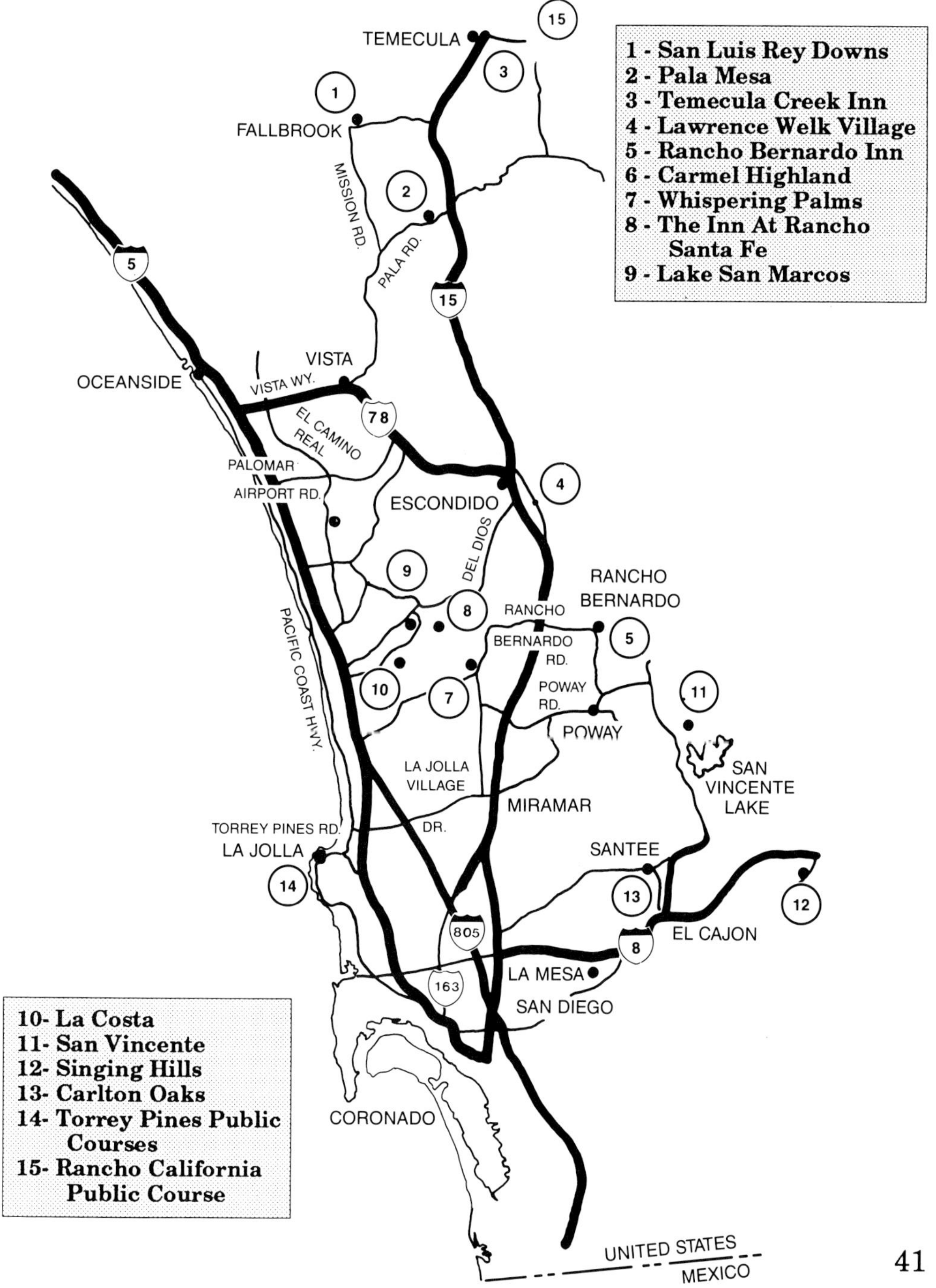

Resorts in the Southern California Desert

1 - The Desert Princess
2 - La Quinta
3 - Cathedral Canyon Resort
4 - Marriott's Desert Springs
5 - Marriott's Rancho Las Palmas
6 - Hyatt Grand Champions Hotel
7 - Stouffer Esmeralda Hotel

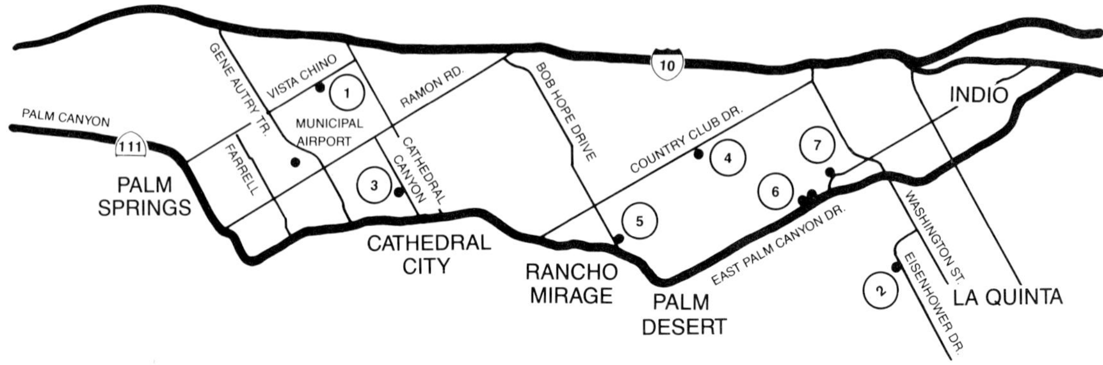

Resorts in the Central Desert

1 - Furnace Creek
2 - Sky Mountain Resort
3 - Rio Bravo at Stallion Springs

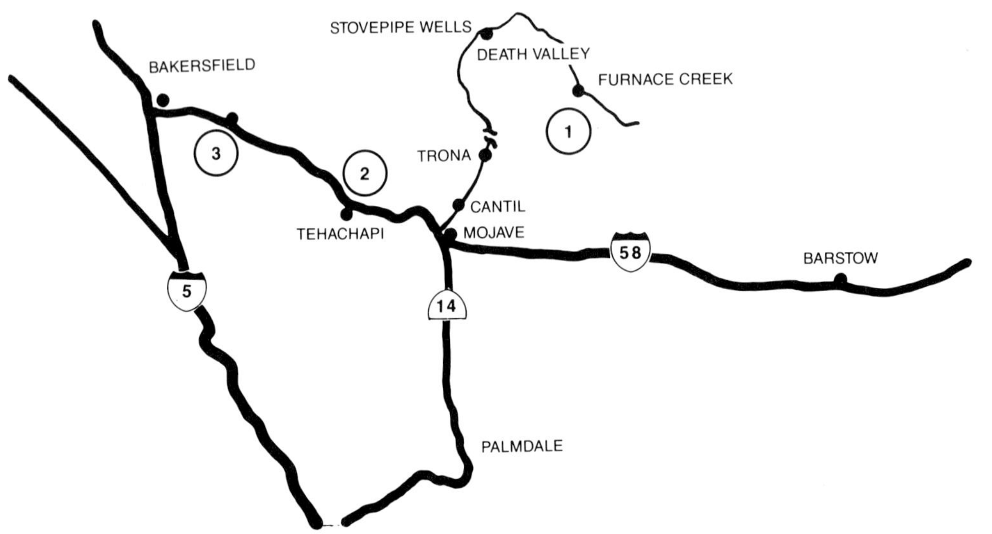

CHAPTER V

Golf Resorts and "notable" public golf courses

Carmel Valley Ranch

Only six miles east of the tourist traffic and beaches at Carmel-by-the-Sea, you'll find this resort where privacy is so paramount, you'll first have to be checked through a gatehouse. Unlike many resorts, Carmel Valley Ranch allows only its members and resort's guests to enjoy its world of luxury and uncrowded pleasures. Impeccably private.

The ranch-style lodge will make you feel like you're in your own private country club. Antiques and early California furnishings, custom woven floral area rugs and wall hangings from local artists, provide the casual, yet luxurious ambience where one can enjoy sunsets suitable for framing.

There are admirable touches in the guest suites, such as Amish comforters, wood burning fireplaces (many suites have two, plus private spas), original water colors, three two-line telephones, security entry system and oversized private decks.

The Spanish-style Tennis Clubhouse was originally built in 1895. Today, after a face-lift, it houses an indoor/outdoor dining area for breakfast, lunch and afternoon cocktails. There are twelve tennis courts, a pool with spa and saunas.

Pete Dye over-extended his creativity when designing this course, taking advantage of the natural terrain. Five holes climb the mountainside, offering fantastic views of the valley floor. There are three man-made lakes, numerous sand and grass bunkers, and lush vegetation to test and challenge different calibers of golfers. Number 9, for example, requires a drive to clear one of the man-made lakes or to land in a narrow strip of fairway with traps in the middle; the balance of this hole is flanked with sand traps on both sides. This is Monterey Peninsula's most meticulously maintained course.

Truly... It's Paradise, golfer's style.

Resort address:
One Old Ranch Rd.
Carmel, CA. 93923
Phone: (408)625-9500
(800)4-CARMEL
Fax: (408)624-2858
No. of rooms: 100
Rates: From $185 to $625
Restaurants: Yes
Business facilities: Yes
Concierge: Yes
Sports facilities: Tennis, swimming, spa.
Dancing: Yes
Baby-sitting: Yes

Course: Carmel Valley
Architect: Pete Dye
Pro: Harry Turner
Statistics: 18-holes, opened in 1980
Yardage/Rating/Slope
Back Tees: 6515/70.1/124
Middle tees: 6055/67.8/119
Front tees: 5088/69.1/132
Guest policy: Private and resort's guests
Dress code: Resort attire
Golf fees: $70
Cart fees: Incl.
Carts on cart path only: 90°rule
Guests carry bags: Yes
Guests pull carts: Yes
Caddies: No
Golf packages: Yes
Pro-shop phone:
(408)626-2510

Location: Hwy. 1 to Carmel Valley Rd.,then South on Robinson Canyon Rd.

Furnace Creek Ranch

The Inn is a Spanish villa-style grande hotel, in the tradition reflecting the elegance and opulence of the 30's. Guests are expected to dress for dinner; "casual elegance" for the ladies and jackets for the men are a must. This requirement is a compliment to the cuisine, exquisitely served in the Main Dining Room. An Italian fare, entertainment and dancing can be enjoyed downstairs in the L'Ottimos restaurant.

While I was relaxing around the swimming pool, I let my imagination wander back to the days when the hardy souls seeking their fortunes came to this valley 205 feet below sea level and named it Death Valley.... Today, most of the action centers around Furnace Creek; surrounded by towering mountains and wrinkled canyons, this resort is like an oasis fed by a mountain spring, evergreen and lush.

This is the world's lowest golf course....It's fun to play, and surprisingly green for an area with minimum rainfall. You don't need a sand wedge in this course, as all bunkers are grass. This is not a long golf course but you'll probably use every club in your bag.

The Resort is only open October through May.

Life after golf ...

Some well known landmark areas worth visiting are Titus Canyon; the Devil's Golf Course, a bed of salt pinnacles, some as high as five feet; Telescope Peak (11,400 feet high), and, directly below it, Badwater, the lowest place in the valley.

The Inn offers tours to Scotty's Castle, once the retreat for an eccentric Midwestern millionaire, now a National Monument. Another site not to be missed are the multicolored hills called Artist's Palette.

There are extensive and panoramic trails to explore on horseback; carriage rides and rentals of 4-wheel vehicles are available. Narrated-sightseeing tours are also available by motorcoach or van.

Resort address:
P.O.Box 1
Death Valley, CA. 92328
Phone: (619)786-2345
Fax: (619)786-2307
No. of rooms: 332
Rates: From $245 to $300
Restaurants: Yes
Business facilities: Yes
Concierge: Yes
Sports facilities: Tennis, horses & bicycles.
Dancing: Yes
Baby-sitting: Yes

Course: Furnace Creek
Architect: William P. Bell
Pro: None
Pro-shop Mgr.: Norm Hedgepeph
Statistics: 18-holes built in 1970
Yardage/Rating/Slope
Back Tees: 5750/66.3/96
Middle tees: None
Front tees: 4977/68.1/99
Guest policy: Resort guests
Dress code: Resort
Golf fees: $25
Cart fees: $25
Carts on cart path only: No
Guests carry bags: Yes
Guests pull carts: Yes
Golf packages: Yes
Pro-shop phone:
(619)786-2301

Location: Hwy.15, exit at Baker and follow Hwy.14/I-395 to Olancha, across the mountains to Hwy.190 to Stove Pipe Wells and Furnace Creek.

Meadowood Resort

Once a private club for celebrated vintners, Meadowood underwent a spectacular change several years ago when fire destroyed the club house. Today, Meadowood is a small luxury resort, an intimate and peaceful gem in the distinctive Victorian-style architecture reminiscent of the Eastern country lodges built at the turn of the century.

The resort has only 70 rooms and suites scattered around 256 acres, offering its guests absolute seclusion from man-made sounds, and absolute privacy.

The new Clubhouse and Conference Center is a sprawling three-story structure that houses Starmont, where the chef prepares classical cuisine; the Fairway Bar and Grill, also in the Center, is a sunny place to greet the day with a Continental breakfast or a full a la carte menu. In addition to the fine restaurants, the Center's golf and croquet shops are also outstanding.

The guest rooms are airy and cheerful, with fans on high beamed ceilings, skylights that open electrically, big white-tiled bathrooms, down comforters, plus thick robes hanging in the closet. The suites have fieldstone fireplaces....very romantic!

There are six championship tennis courts, a large swimming pool and hiking and biking trails; at the regulation English croquet courts, Damon Bindencope, a top competitor with the 1986 Australian Croquet Team teaches all levels and games.

The executive golf course is fun to play and also challenging. It's so quiet... one really feels like whispering: "fore"....

I would also suggest asking the Concierge to arrange for a starting-time at the Chardonnay Club, a unique Scottish design 27-hole championship public course set on 368 acres of natural rolling hills, with grassy mounds and bunkers surrounding every green. The course is interlaced with vinyards, lakes and streams.

...continued on page 117

Resort address:
900 Meadowood Lane
St. Helena, Ca. 94574
Phone: (800)458-8080
(707)963-3646
Fax: (707)963-3532
No. of rooms: 70
Rates: From $200.00 to $535.00
Restaurants: Yes
Business facilities: Yes
Concierge: Yes
Sports facilities: Tennis, croquet, swimming, biking.
Dancing: No
Baby-sitting: No

Course: Meadowood
Architect: Unknown
Pro: Joe Roberts
Statistics: 9-holes (executive) opened in 1963
Yardage/Rating/Slope
Back Tees: 4130/61/92
Middle tees: None
Front tees: 4126/60.9/92
Guest policy: Resort guests and members only
Dress code: Strict resort
Golf fees: $25
Cart fees: $3
Carts on cart path only: No
Guests carry bags: Yes
Guests pull carts: Yes
Golf packages: No
Pro-shop phone:
(707)963-3646

Location: North on Interstate 80, across the Carquinez Bridge and past Vallejo. Exit at Highway 37 and drive into the valley. Take Oak-Knoll Rd. to Meadowood.

Quail Lodge Resort and Golf Club

Thirty years ago, Ed Harber and thirty other local residents acquired the Carmel Valley Dairy, promising the original owners, the Charles Lindberg and the Dwight Morrow families, that the ecological beauty of the property would always be respected. To fulfill that promise when the dairies went out of business, they decided to use the land for a golf resort.

Quail Lodge is a fine resort and a place of serenity. There are eleven lakes serving as wildlife sanctuaries. Migrating fowl come to visit there every year. The President's Animal Farm shelters horses, burros, sheep, Scottish Highland cattle and Andalusian goats (Cleveland Armory talked the Harbers into sheltering these so they could be saved from destruction at their natural habitat in the one of the Santa Barbara islands). Deer also roam the course, along with the quails, duck and geese who glide over the lakes and ponds.

One can enjoy a picnic and a spectacular view of the Pacific Ocean and Carmel by hiking to the ridge of the property. Others might enjoy trout fishing in the private lake.

Ben Doyle, who has been the golf pro at the club since 1973, still offers free lessons to members and lodge guests. Bobby Clampett, who grew up in Carmel Valley, was Doyle's star pupil. Other sports available include tennis, swimming, croquet, ping-pong, and bicycling.

Only members and Lodge guests enjoy this perfectly maintained and challenging course. The men and the ladies each have their separate score cards....Unique, n'est-ce pas?

The Quail Lodge has been the recipient (for ten of the last twelve years) of the much coveted Mobil Travel Guide Five-Star Award.

Resort address:
8205 Valley Greens Dr.
Phone: (408)624-1581
(800)538-9516 outside CA.
(800)682-9303 in CA.
Fax: (408) 624-3726
No. of rooms: 100
Rates: From $185 to $830
Restaurants: Yes
Business facilities: Yes
Concierge: Yes
Sports facilities: Several
Dancing: No
Baby-sitting: No

Course: Carmel Valley Golf and C.C.
Architect: Robert Muir Graves
Pro: Ben Doyle
Statistics: 18-holes opened in 1963
Yardage/Rating/Slope
Back Tees: 6141/69.7/126
Middle tees: N/A
Front tees: 5453/71.6/122
Guest policy: Members & Lodge guests
Reciprocal privileges also.
Dress code: Resort attire
Golf fees: $70
Others: $90
Cart fees: Incl.
Carts on cart path only: No
Guests carry bags: No
Guests pull carts: No
Golf packages: Yes
Pro-shop phone: (408)624-1581

Location: Hwy.1 to Carmel Valley Rd.. Drive 3.4 miles to Lodge's entrance.

Rancho Murieta Country Club

This charming country community bordering the banks of the Cosumnes River encompasses five lakes, two eighteen hole championship golf courses, jogging trails, bike paths, lighted tennis courts, and sandy beaches. The area itself is a private game preserve that is home to a variety of wildlife.... all this only 24 miles east of downtown Sacramento.

The North Course was redesigned in 1972 by Arnold Palmer and is a true test of golf. A variety of golf events are hosted here, including the popular Senior PGA Tour.

The South Course was completed in 1978 and designed by Ted Robinson. This course is kinder, but by no means a "pushover."

This is a small but extremely comfortable and friendly resort. The accommodations are spacious, with most of them overlooking the 18th fairway.

> ***"At Le Golf du Medoc, a course near Bordeaux, France, all 18 holes are named after a vineyard in the region. The 18th hole is called Mouton Rothschild, and anyone who makes a hole-in-one on the 5th hole, Pontet Canet, wins an imperial bottle of wine."***
>
> — Golf Digest, May 1990

Resort address:
14813 Jackson Rd.
Rancho Murieta, CA. 95683
Phone: (916)985-7200
(800)852-GOLF
Fax: (916)354-0916
No. of rooms: 74
Rates: From $45 to $115
Restaurants: Yes
Business facilities: Yes
Concierge: No
Sports facilities: Tennis, swimming, jogging, biking
Dancing: No
Baby-sitting: No

Courses: The North & The South
Architect: ***North:*** Arnold Palmer
South: Ted Robinson
Pro: David Hall
Statistics: 36-holes
Yardage/Rating/Slope
North:
Back Tees: 6875/73.3/129
Middle tees: 6371/71.1/122
Front tees: 5642/72.8/128
South:
Back Tees: 6886/72.2/124
Middle tees: 6307/70.2/118
Front tees: 5527/71.5/118
Guest policy: Lodge guests & Members
Dress code: Resort
Golf fees: Weekdays: $65
Weekends: $75
Cart fees: Included
Carts on cart path only: Seasonal
Guests carry bags: No
Guests pull carts: No
Golf packages: Yes
Pro-shop phone: (916)985-7200

Location: From Sacramento go east on Hwy. 50, turn south on Bradshaw Rd, then left on Jackson Rd.

Silverado

Dating back to the early 1870s, this mansion was originally the home of Maj. Gen. John Franklin Miller, the Civil War hero who later on became a U.S. Senator. Eventually, in 1953, the property was sold to the former golf-pro Pat Markovich. In 1955, the Silverado Golf Course was opened for play. But in 1966, Robert Trent Jones redesigned the entire layout to what it is today: The North and the South Courses, each consisting of 18-championship-holes.

The North Course is the kinder of the two. The South Course is more exciting, tougher, and by far the more picturesque. The toughest hole is #8, dogleg right with a strategically placed bunker in front. The grand finale is the 500 yard, par 5, dogleg left with a bunker waiting for you at the bend. And to quote Jeff Goodwin, "the green is guarded by what you are sure is the Sahara Desert."

Silverado's three restaurants offer diversified cuisine. The Royal Oak serves a wonderful hearty fare of mesquite steak, lobster, and lamb in a country atmosphere. The Vintner's Court serves California cuisine in an elegant and romantic setting. The wines served in both restaurants are strictly Napa Valley.

You are in the heart of the Wine Country... so what better way to spend your apres golf hours than visiting some of the famous Napa wineries? The hotel will arrange for tours and an elegant boxed picnic to help you enjoy your wine-tasting adventure.

"If you are going to be in the limelight, you might as well dress for it."
—Jimmy Demaret

Resort address:
1600 Atlas Peak Rd.
Napa, CA. 94558
Phone: (707)257-0200
(800)532-0500
Fax: (704)257-5400
No.of rooms: 269
Rates: From $130 to $465
Restaurants: Yes
Business facilities: Yes
Concierge: Yes
Sports facilities: Tennis, swimming
Dancing: Yes
Baby-sitting: Yes

Courses: Siverado's North & South
Architect: Robert Trent Jones
Pro: Jeff Goodwin
Statistics: 36-holes opened in 1956
Yardage/Rating/Slope
South Course:
Back-Tees: 6632/71.7/127
Middle-tees: 6213/69.6/123
Front-tees: 5672/71.8/123
North Course:
Back Tees: 6896/73.0/131
Middle-tees: 6351/70.3/126
Front-tees: 5857/73.9/124
Guest policy: Hotel guest & Members
Dress code: Resort attire
Golf fees: $70 (Hotel guests) Others $85
Cart fees: Incl.
Carts on cart path only: Yes
Guests carry bags: No
Guests pull carts: No
Golf packages: Yes
Pro-shop phone:
(707)257-0200

...continued on page 117

The Inn at Spanish Bay

This is an exquisite addition to the famed Monterey Peninsula, which is internationally renowned and indisputably one of the most spectacular settings in the world.

This resort stands at the edge of the Del Monte Forest, approached by the fabled 17-Mile Drive, only 300 yards from the Pacific shore, and completely surrounded by the classic linksland golf course, reminiscent of Scotland's finest.

The Links at Spanish Bay is characterized by rolling fairways and huge sand dunes, up to 24 feet in height... Most fairways and greens are exposed to the prevailing winds off the Pacific Ocean. But there are also the more sheltered fairways winding through the Del Monte forest.

The interior design of the Inn is casual, yet elegant and luxurious. An enormous fireplace in the lobby was built of Del Monte stone, quarried nearby. Kotah stone flooring and walnut paneling are the backgrounds for the elegant furnishings adorning the Lounge. The rooms and suites are equally luxurious. Each has its own sofas and oversized chairs in a living room grouping in front of the fireplace, quilted down comforter, separate dressing rooms, baths finished in Italian marble, and limited-edition artwork decorating the walls. Three expansive suites have grand pianos, exotic flowering plants, and objets d'art. And from every window or balcony, one feasts their eyes on a spectacular landscape of sparkling surf, and fiery sunsets.

Dining is formal and elegant at The Bay Club, where the cuisine is Northern Italian. Breakfast, lunch and dinner are served on a seafront alfresco terrace, The Dunes, which offers candlelight and the romantic notes of a grand piano. The menu is classically Californian. Traps features nightly entertainment, and the Lobby Lounge is an inviting place to enjoy cocktails overlooking the second green.

As a guest of The Inn at Spanish Bay, one can also enjoy playing Pebble Beach Golf Links, Spyglass Hill Golf Course, and Del Monte, the oldest golf course still in operation west of the Mississippi (built in 1897).

...continued on page 117

Resort address:
2700 17-Mile Dr.
Pebble Beach, CA. 93953
Phone: (408)647-7500
Fax: (408)647-7443
No. of rooms: 270
Rates: From $220 to $1,400 (15% gratuity will be added to final bill)
Restaurants: Several
Business facilities: Several
Concierge: Yes
Sports facilities: Tennis, Swimming, Spa
Dancing: Yes
Baby-sitting: No

Course: The Links at Spanish Bay
Architects: Tom Watson, Robert Trent Jones, Jr. and Frank "Sandy" Tatum.
Pro: George Price
Statistics: 18-holes, completed in 1985
Yardage/Rating/Slope
Back Tees: 6820/74.7/144
Middle tees: 6078/70.8/133
Front tees: 5287/70.8/120
Guest policy: Resort guests and Public
Dress code: Resort attire
Golf fees: Resort guests:$75 Others: $115
Cart fees: Incl.
Caddies: Yes $30 per bag
Carts on cart path only: Yes
Guests carry bags: Yes
Guests pull carts: No
Golf packages: No
Pro-shop phone: (408)624-3811

...continued on page 117

The Lodge at Pebble Beach

Originally built in 1919, The Lodge was known for the next 58 years as The Del Monte Lodge. In 1977, the hotel's name was changed to The Lodge at Pebble Beach.

Among its 161 rooms, eleven are in the original, beautifully renovated main building; the others are in several low-rise buildings hidden throughout the six-acre grounds and golf links. My favorite suites overlook the 18th fairway, where you can enjoy the sunset from your balcony, occasionally hear the bark of sea lions, and enjoy a drink from the well-stocked honor-system bar in front of a stone fireplace stacked daily with oak and pine logs.

Upscale amenities such as baths with separate dressing areas, terry robes, and twice-a-day maid service are only a few of the many elegant touches you'll encounter as a guest of The Lodge.

Your stay at The Lodge must include a visit to The Tap Room, where the decor includes a fascinating collection of golf memorabilia, including photos from the "Crosby" and the 1972 and 1982 U.S.Open Championships. The menu offers a selection of English pub specialties.

One cannot ignore Club XIX, which changes from a sunny daytime sidewalk cafe into a romantic and elegant French terrace at night.

The Beach and Tennis Club is located is located along Stillwater Cove, with 14 tennis courts and a heated swimming pool overlooking the surf. At the Equestrian Center, guests can "mount up" and set out over 34 miles of bridle paths weaving into the Del Monte Forest.

The golf course swings back and forth along the coast for holes 4 through 10, then moves inland, returning to the shoreline for the 17th and the famous 18th, which is a narrow strip of land running between the main building and the bay. The 8th is a masochistic challenge to the average golfer, who, assuming he or she has a good drive, will have to somehow negotiate the next shot over 100-foot-high cliffs. But cheer up; eventually one of your next shots will land on the green.

...continued on page 117

Resort address:
Pebble Beach, CA. 93953
Phone: (800)654-9300
Fax: (408)624-6357
No. of rooms: 161
Rates: From $265 to $1,800
Restaurants: Several
Business facilities: Several
Concierge: Yes
Sports facilities: Tennis, swimming, equestrian.
Dancing: Yes
Baby-sitting: No

Course: Pebble Beach Golf Links
Architect: Jack Neville
Pro: R.J. Harper
Statistics: 18-holes built in 1919
Yardage/Rating/Slope
Back Tees: 6799/75.0/144
Middle tees: 6357/72.7/139
Front tees: 5197/70.3/139
Guest policy: Resort guests and public
Dress code: Resort attire
Golf fees: Lodge guests: $125 (all others $175)
Cart fees: Incl.
Carts on cart path only: Yes
Guests carry bags: No
Guests pull carts: No
Caddies: Yes $30/bag
Golf packages: No
Pro-shop phone:
(408)624-6611

Location: Hwy. 101 to the Monterey Penninsula turn-off, 156 west, to Hwy.1 south to the 17-Mile Dr./Pebble Beach exit. A guard at the entrance gate will direct you to the resort.

Spyglass Hill Golf Course

The story goes that Robert Louis Stevenson received inspiration for his 1883 Treasure Island while visiting the Monterey Peninsula. And it is believed that he wrote by the hour, while sitting atop a hill overlooking Monterey Bay, close to the site that is now the course's clubhouse. Consistent with the course's title, names taken from Stevenson's classic fantasy were given to the 18-holes.

Examples:

#1 - Treasure Island... this first green is an island in the sand.

#2 - The Black Spot... The choices are: hit the green or the sand.

#14 - Long John River... Double dog leg, par 5, that you'll always remember.

#15 - Jim Hawkins... The only kindly hole in the course.

#16 - Black Dog... scurrilous at best. Few players can cope with this long and infamous par 4 (465 yards).

In short, Spyglass Hill is rated an unforgiving, challenging, thoroughly professional course, requiring a caliber of play equal to that of Pebble Beach.

Course: Spyglass Hill
Architect: Robert Trent Jones, Sr.
Pro: Laird Small
Statistics: 18-holes, opened in 1966
Yardage/Rating/Slope
Back Tees: 6810/76.1/141
Middle tees: 6277/73.1/135
Front tees: 5556/72.8/131
Guest policy: Resort guests and public
Dress code: Resort attire
Golf fees: $95 Resort guests (all others $115)
Cart fees: Incl.
Carts on cart path only: Yes
Guests carry bags: Yes
Guests pull carts: Yes
Caddies: Yes $30/bag
Golf packages: Yes
Pro-shop phone: (408)624-3811

Location: Hwy.101 to the Monterey Penninsula turn-off, 156 west, to Hwy.1 south to the 17-Mile Dr./Pebble Beach exit. A guard at the entrance gate will direct you to the golf

Black Lake Golf Resort

This golf course is the gem of the Central Coast. The course is rated in the top 25 of California resorts. Fully equipped Condominiums only, not rooms are rented by the night, week or month. A coffee shop serves breakfast and lunch only.

Here, there is no life after golf...Dinner cooked in your own condo may be the best meal in town. But, golf alone makes this a very worth while stop during your golfing vacation.

Take a good look at the drawings in the score card before playing each hole. There are lots of surprises ahead. The 1st hole is a par 3, with a very narrow fairway and big trees on either side. As a matter of fact, it appears to me that the fairways get narrower and narrower as the game progresses. Black Lake's No. 6, par 5 leaves you in the middle of the fairway after your drive, with a sightless attempt for your second shot. Because it's a par 5 the automatic reaction is to reach for a wood. Don't... A lake wraps around the 6th green from the front to the back. A lay up shot would be the smart choice. The 11th hole is a par 5, with a tee shot over a barranca. A driver may put you through the fairway into the trees.

This is an exciting golf course, and whether well or poorly played, you'll finish the round exhilarated. Black Lake is rated in the top twenty five California golf resorts, three years running.

Resort address:
1490 Golf Course Lane
Nipomo,CA. 93444
Phone: (805)343-1718
(800)423-0981
FAX: No
No.of condominiums: 46
Rates: From $89/ $144
Business facilities: No
Sports facilities: No
Dancing: No

Course: Black Lake: 18-holes, opened in 1985
Designer: Ted Robinson
Pro: Dan Stills
Yardage/Rating/Slope
Back Tees: 6427/70.0/121
Middle tees: 6027/68.9/114
Front tees: 5614/71.8/122
Guest policy: Resort guests and public
Dress code: Reasonable golf attire
Golf fees:
Weekdays: $15
Weekends: $30
Cart fees:
Weekdays: $18
Weekends: $20
Carts on cart path only:
90°rule applies
Caddies: No
Guests carry bags: No
Guests pull carts: No
Golf packages: Yes
Pro-shop phone:
(805)481-4204

Location:
Hwy 101, turn off on Tefft Rd., go West. On Pomeroy turn right to Willow Road.

The Alisal Guest Ranch

I'll always remember The Alisal Guest Ranch for the friendly, casual and comfortable atmosphere. The staff has been there for years; they know how to make the ranch work for the guest's pleasure.

This is an upscale ranch-resort, near Santa Barbara, in the Santa Inez Valley in the Danish community of Solvang. Originally a cattle ranch, in 1946 it became "The Alisal" with only 30 rooms. It was an immediate success.

Horseback riding though unbelievable beautiful trails where deer graze, fishing or sailing in the 100-acre lake, playing tennis (the tennis Pro will always make sure you have a game) or golf in the immaculately kept golf course, keep guests from all over the country coming back year after year.

Clark Gable married Lady Sylvia in the Alisal's old library. The movie stars still come. Although The Alisal today maintains a very low profile, the quality and comfort are always visible.

The Ranch operates on a modified American Plan, including breakfast and dinner in the cost of a 2-night minimum stay. The rooms and suites are in small bungalows, designed in the tradition of the Old West. There are no televisions or telephones in any of the rooms. Only one television exists in the Recreation Room, and public telephones are available outside the lobby.

Golf is wonderful... 18-holes of manicured undulated fairways and greens surrounded by old sycamore and oak trees, lots of hills, and creeks weaving through the fairways when you least expect them... all seem designed to create havoc with your game. A good score in this course is the result of a game very well played. The 9th is a mean par 3, requiring an absolutely straight shot to the green. Nothing else will do.... The 17th has a creek running across the fairway just short of the average drive. Stay to the right of the fairway or your shot to the green will be blocked by the beautiful sycamores.

Resort address:
1054 Alisal Rd.
Solvang, CA. 93463
Phone: (805)688-6411
Fax: (805)688-2510
No. of rooms: 69
Rates: From $225 to $280
Restaurants: Yes
Business facilities: Yes
Concierge: No
Sports facilities: Tennis, equestrian, windsurfing and fishing
Dancing: Yes
Baby-sitting: Yes

Course: The Alisal
Architect: William Bell
Pro: John Hardy
Statistics: 18-holes opened in 1946
Yardage/Rating/Slope
Back Tees: 6286/70.0/121
Middle tees: 5919/71.9/114
Front tees: 5594/71.9/123
Guest policy: Members and Resort guests only
Dress code: Strict resort attire
Golf fees: $25
Cart fees: 18
Carts on cart path only: No
Guests carry bags: Yes
Guests pull carts: Yes
Golf packages: Yes
Pro-shop phone:
(805)688-2510

Location: Hwy. 101, take the exit to Solvang. Drive through Solvang and turn right on Alisal Rd.

Horse Thief Country Club at Sky Mountain Resort

The beauty, peace and quiet of the Tehachapi Mountains create the perfect backdrop for this elegant four-season resort perched at 4,000 feet, and surrounded by thousand of ancient oak trees.

The Sky Mountain Lodge has recently been refurbished in a colorful Southwestern theme admirably suited to the surrounding environment.

Although golfing is the focal point of this Resort, this is a family getaway that has everything for everyone. There are the fully equipped Equestrian Center, basketball, sand volleyball and tennis courts, croquet, shuffleboard, an 18-hole miniature golf course, an eight-lane bowling alley and an outdoor amphitheater for plays and puppet shows. If this isn't enough, there are 4,600 acres of riding and hiking trails.

The golf course is outstanding! Number 7 is the most picturesque hole. The tee sits 70'over water, above the green, giving the impression of hitting through a chute. There's also a bunker in front of a very undulated green. Joe Haggety, the PGA Professional at the Resort, likes number 3 best: "your drive has to carry 150 yards over water, then there's a lake that runs on the right side of this dog-leg-right fairway, with O.B. on the left. The second shot will be from a down hill lie which could put the average golfer's ball in the water. It's a tough hole...."

Horse Thief is a resort where one forgets the world they've left behind.

> ***"Sports do not build character, they reveal it."***
>
> — Heywood Hale Broun

Resort address:
Star Route 1, Box 2931
Tehachapi, CA.93561
Phone: (805)822-5581
(800)367-0470
Fax: (805)822-4055
No. of rooms: 99
Rates: From $65.00 to $200.00
Restaurants: Yes
Business facilities: Yes
Concierge: No
Sports facilities: Several (see resort description)
Dancing: Yes
Baby-sitting: Yes

Course: Horse Chief C.C.
Architect: Robert Baldock
Pro: Joe Haggety
Statistics: 18-holes completed in 1974
Yardage/Rating/Slope
Back Tees: 6650/72.1/129
Middle tees: 6317/70.1/121
Front tees: 5723/66.9/116/116
Guest policy: Resort guests and public
Dress code: Resort attire
Golf fees:
Weekdays: $15.00
Weekends: $25.00
Cart fees: $18.00
Carts on cart path only: No
Guests carry bags: Yes
Guests pull carts: Yes
Golf packages: Yes
Pro-shop phone:
(805)822-5581, ext.221

Location: Hwy.58 to Tehachapi. Exit at Route 202 off-ramp in Tehachapi and follow the signs to Sky Mountain at Stallion Springs.

Ojai Valley Inn and Country Club

Ojai Valley Inn & C.C was completely remodeled in 1988. The old resort was demolished and replaced with new spacious and elegant haciendas depicting the Spanish-California architecture.

Ojai was the location for Shangri-la in the film Lost Horizon.

Today, the valley still reflects the image of the genteel Southern California lifestyle of the early part of this century, when comfort and elegance reign.

The golf course was originally designed by Billy Bell and George C. Thomas Jr. in 1924. Recently Jay Morrish, known for his designs of the TPC and Troon Courses in Scottsdale, redesigned the greens, tees, and sand traps, and added a modern drainage system to provide a very challenging golf course while preserving the masterwork of the past.

All the 218 rooms are spacious and thoughtfully stocked with mini bars and comfortable terry cloth robes. Fifteen suites have fireplaces. Most rooms look over the golf course and surrounding mountains with spectacular sunsets.

Lunch "under the oaks" on the terrace is an Ojai tradition and a candlelight dinner is served in the Vista Dining room. For a more casual but equally rewarding culinary experience try the Oak Grill.

Children are always welcome at the Inn. During the holiday peak periods the small guests are invited to western cookouts and a counselor is available to entertain them. Tennis, bicycles, swings, a sand box, jungle gym, horseshoes and croquet are accessible to them.

After golf enjoy tennis on one of the eight courts (four lighted for night play) or swim in the 60-foot lap pool next to the fitness center, exercise room and spa. Trails for jogging and bicycling connect the Inn to the nearby village.

Resort address:
Country Club Rd.
Ojai, CA. 93023
Phone: (805)646-5511
(800)422-OJAI
Fax: (805)646-7969
No. of rooms: 218
Estimated rates: From $180 to $680
Baby sitting: Yes
Business facilities: Yes
Concierge: Yes
Sports facilities: Several
Dancing: Yes

Course: Ojai Country Club
Architect: George Thomas Jr. and Wm. Bell
Renovation Architect:
Jay Morrish
Pro: Scott Flynn
Statistics: 18-holes, opened in 1923
Yardage/Rating/Slope
Back Tees: 6252/70.6/123
Middle tees: 5909/68.9/117
Front tees: 5242/70.0/121
Guest policy: Resort guests & Members
Dress code: Resort attire
Golf fees:
Weekdays $60
Weekends $65
Cart fees: $24
Carts on cart path only: No
Caddies: No
Guests carry bags: Yes
Guests pull carts: Yes
Golf packages: Yes
Pro-shop phone:
(805)646-2420

Location: Hwy 101 exit on Hwy 33 to Ojai.

The Radisson Suite Hotel At River Ridge

In the summertime, you'll be able to glimpse the Raiders' training camp while waiting to tee off on the 8th and 9th holes. You may even luck out and get a game with one of the "hulks" (I wonder if Bo plays golf).

This course is challenging due to winds, rolling terrain and water. On the first hole you'll hit off an elevated tee over a gully and probably land on a side hill lie, where you'll hit to an elevated green. The second hole is an easy hole that should restore your "golfing ego." The most difficult hole in the front nine has to be the 4th. It's about 600 yds from the back tee and 540 yds from the front tee with a narrow fairway that has O/B on the left, but straight on to the green.

The back nine is longer, with lots of water hazards and constant heavy winds in the afternoon. Water is prevalent on holes 11 through 14, which is a par 3 with an island green.

The Radisson Suites are around the golf course and come complete with kitchens and sitting areas, a few have fireplaces. Complimentary breakfast is served at Mullarkey's, the hotel's dining room.

There are five lighted tennis courts, two swimming pools, hot tubs and health facilities. On weekends there's the Comedy Outlet, where the price of admission is included if you dine at Mullarkcy's.

> ***"I believe the real reason St. Andrews Old Course is infinitely superior to anything else is owing to the fact that it was constructed when no one knew anything about the subject at all."***
>
> — Dr. Alister Mackenzie,
> "Golf Architecture" (1920)

Resort address:
2101 West Vineyard Ave.
Oxnard, CA. 93030
Phone: (805)988-0130
(800)333-3333
Fax: (805)983-4470
No. of rooms: 253
Estimated rates: From $90 to $130
Restaurants: Yes
Business facilities: No
Concierge: Yes
Sports facilities: Tennis, health, pool
Dancing: No

Course: River Ridge
Architect: Billy Bell
Pro: Marc Sippes
Statistics: 18-holes, built in 1986
Yardage/Rating/Slope
Back Tees: 6543/70.7/114
Middle tees: 6111/68.7/109
Front tees: 5525/72.0/116
Guest policy: Public & Resort guests
Dress code: Casual
Golf fees:
Weekday: $12
Weekend: $14
Cart fees: $16
Carts on cart path only: No
Caddies: No
Guests carry bags: Yes
Guests pull carts: Yes
Golf packages: Yes
Pro-shop phone:
(805)983-GOLF

Location: Hwy.101 exit on Vineyard.

Rio Bravo Golf and Tennis Club

Rio Bravo appeals to the golfer who wants to relax and unwind, as well as the golfer who wants to pursue some vigorous exercise such as river rafting and kayaking after 18-holes. Am I serious? Of course.... A non-golfing family would really appreciate this resort and its surrounding activities.

Guests are encouraged to bring their own equipment to water-ski, windsurf, or sail the waters of the 110 acre Lake Ming, adjoining the Resort. If fishing appeals to you, Kern River Canyon is periodically stocked with trout.... At Kern River one can tackle the challenging rapids in a raft or a kayak, if you really know what you're doing.

Rio Bravo is on the "ten best" lists of Tennis Magazine and California Golf Journal. Among its many distinctions, the golf course has been the site of the Southern California Open since 1986 and the PGA Tour Regional Qualifying Tournament since 1987.

The front nine holes are flat, and the back nine is hilly. It's like playing two different courses. I asked Jerry Steenerson, the resort's PGA Professional, which hole he considered the toughest: "the eleventh, because it's an all up-hill par 5, 616 yds. from the blue tees. There aren't any bunkers along the fairway nor many flat lies.... plus an undulating quick green, very difficult to read." When asked about his favorite hole, Jerry cites number 14, a dog-leg-right, narrow and flanked by trees.

The resort's accommodations are spacious and comfortable. The resort's restaurant, Godfreys, is reknown for their tender and juicy steaks which come from the midwest.

Local transportation to and from the airport and AMTRAC station is provided by the resort's courtesy van.

The golf course is closed on Tuesdays. Although the course is open year-round there's a definite possibility of frost in December and January, and July and August are unbearably hot.

Resort address:
11200 Lake Ming Rd.
Bakersfield, CA. 93306
Phone: (805)872-5000
(800)282-5000
Fax: No
No. of rooms: 110
Rates: From $68 to $234
Restaurants: Yes
Business facilities: Yes
Concierge: No
Sports facilities: Tennis, pool, gym, volleyball and basketball
Dancing: Yes
Baby-sitting: Yes

Course: Rio Bravo
Architect: Robert Muir Graves
Pro: Jerry Steenerson
Statistics: 18-holes, built in 1981
Yardage/Rating/Slope
Back Tees: 7018/74.4/138
Middle tees: 6555/70.9/122
Front tees: 5704/72.2/120
Guest policy: Private and Resort guests
Dress code: Strict Resort attire
Golf fees: $39
Cart fees: Incl.
Carts on cart path only: 90°rule
Guests carry bags: No
Guests pull carts: No
Golf packages: Yes
Pro-shop phone: (805)871-4653

Location: Hwy.58 to Comanche Rd. exit (East), right to Lake Ming Rd.

La Purisima Golf Course

This is a championship public golf course deserving of mention in this book and certainly worth playing during your golfing vacation. It is situated in the Lompoc Valley, near the Danish Village of Solvang. The Sheraton Royal in Solvang offers very attractive golf packages at La Purisima.

La Purisima was designed by Robert Muir Graves in 1986 to meet the requirements of major PGA and LPGA tournaments. One word describes La Purisima: "tough!" The synergy of its uneven terrain, natural obstacles, water, length and wind combined add up to a very challenging course. By the way, the wind comes up around noon.

As an example of the course's length, I'll mention the 12th hole, par 5, 609 yds. This hole is a "4 shot"to the green for most golfers. Holes 3-4-14 and 17 require "finesse." The fairways are sloped with blind tee shots on nos. 4, 2 and 14. The 3rd and 17th holes have very shallow greens, making distance judgment critical. Both holes have water in front and a hillside behind the greens. Most greens are fast and undulated.

Course address:
3455 State Hwy.24
Lompoc, CA. 93436
Phone: (805)735-8395
Fax: (805)736-0246
Coffee shop: Yes
Services: Driving range, putting green
Architect: Robert Muir Graves
Pro: Tom Ringer
Statistics: Built in 1986
Yardage/Rating/Slope
Back Tees: 7105/75.5/142
Middle tees: 6657/72.2/132
Front tees: 5763/73.3/131
Guest policy: Public
Dress code: Golf attire
Golf fees:
Weekday $30
Weekend $40
Cart fees: $22
Carts on cart path only: No
Caddies: No
Guests carry bags: No
Guests pull carts: No
Golf packages: Yes

Location: Hwy.101, exit on Hwy.24 to Lompoc. Aprox. 5 miles to golf course.

Sandpiper Golf Course

Sandpiper is one of the most picturesque public golf courses in California. Three fairways run along the ocean and two other greens sit high on bluffs overlooking the Pacific.In many ways I find Sandpiper to be as scenic as Pebble Beach, and a lot easier on the pocketbook.

Designed by Billy Bell in 1971, Sandpiper has hosted several PGA and LPGA tournaments, the most recently beeing the LPGA in 1989.

It's not easy to get starting times; you must call seven days in advance. Do it! It's definitely worth your vacation time...

My favorite hole is No.11, par 3, it has an elevated tee with a fabulous view of the ocean behind the green, which is surrounded by sand-traps. For some strange reason, it's hard to hit on the green. I think the "Golf Fairy" likes to remind us that golf is a humbling game. On No. 13, par 5, one has to have an accurate third shot to the elevated green; otherwise you'll find yourself at the bottom of a ravine and then... I have no idea what you'll do. ... I've been there and I don't want to remember.

Course address:
7925 Hollister Ave.
Goleta, CA. 93117
Phone: (805)968-1541
Coffee Shop: Yes
Architect: Billy Bell
Pro: John Hughes
Statistics: 18-holes opened in
Yardage/Rating/Slope
Back Tees: 7053/74.7/135
Middle tees: 6645/71.3/126
Front tees: 5766/72.6/117
Guest policy: Public
Dress code: Golf attire
Golf fees:
Weekdays $40
Weekends: $60
Cart fees: $22
Carts on cart path only: No
Caddies: No
Guests carry bags: Yes
Guests pull carts: Yes
Golf packages: No

Location: Hwy.101, exit on Winchester Canyon Rd. to Hollister.

Carmel Highland Resort

The old Rancho Penasquitos Golf Course... by any other name, definitely not the same...

The resort architecture is contemporary. The interior design is trendy Southwestern. The exterior is bright pink... a standout in the casual atmosphere of the North San Diego County.

All the rooms are spacious and overlook the golf course. There are six wind-protected tennis courts, three of them lighted for night play in addition to two heated pools, steam and massage rooms.

The golf course is now Carmel Valley. Totally refurbished with more bunkers and water hazards than before.

"The meat of the course is No. 2 through No. 8 holes. If the golfer manages to shoot par, then he may have a slim chance at a decent round," says Michael Flanagan, the resident PGA professional.

One of the toughest holes is the 8th, par 4, plays like a par-5. Its 458 yards into a strong prevailing wind, and a steep incline require length and accuracy due to the bunkers on both sides of the fairway plus the sloping green, which is also bunkered.

"A shepherd tending his sheep would often chance upon a round pebble, and having his crook in his hand, he would strike it away; for it is inevitable that a man with a stick in his hand should aim a blow at any loose object in his path as that he should breathe."

—Sir Walter Simpson, from his book, "The Art of Golf" (1887)

Resort address:
1455 Penasquitos Rd.
San Diego, CA. 92129
Phone: (619)672-9100
(800)622-9223
Fax: (619)672-9166
No. of rooms: 176
Estimated rates: $90/$230
Business facilities: Yes
Sports facilities: Tennis, swimming.
Dancing: Yes
Baby-sitting: Yes

Course: Carmel Highland
Designer: Not known
Pro: Mike Flanagan
Statistics: 18-holes opened in 1967
Yardage/Rating/Slope
BackTees: 6501/71.1/122
Middle tees: 6108/68.9/11
Front tees: 5488/71.4/119
Guest policy: Resort Guests and public
Dress code: Casual
Golf fees:
Weekday $25
Weekend $39 (incl. cart)
Cart fees: $18
Carts on cart path only: No
Caddies: No
Guests carry bags: Yes (Weekdays only)
Guests pull carts: Yes (Weekdays only)
Golf packages: Yes
Pro-shop phone:
(619) 672-2200

Location: I-15 Exit at Carmel Mountain Rd. and go West 1/4 mile to Penasquitos Rd.

Cathedral Canyon Resort

The keys to playing this course are patience and accuracy...in short, good course "management."

Missing any greens in this course could be hazardous to your score. Hybrid Bermuda grass greens (great for early birds and late day golfers) are well guarded by trees, water and bunkers.

This is a mature golf course that has undergone major changes since its opening in 1974. The course now has twenty two lakes and at least sixty eight bunkers.

The 1st hole is a very tough par 5, dogleg to the right with two lakes crossing the fairway. Number 9, is one of the most beautiful par 3's in the desert. The 14th hole has three lakes: one on the right side of the fairway on the drive, another waiting to catch a hook on the second shot, and the third guarding the front and right sides of the green. Add two green-side bunkers, and the result is an opening ten feet wide through which to thread a short shot.

A new 9 hole course is expected to open by mid 1990.

The resort is friendly. A two-story, Spanish style hotel features suites with views of the golf course. Pool-side dining and an intimate lounge with a piano bar conclude the day.

> ***"Golf matches are not won on the fairways or greens. They're won on the tee. The first tee."***
> — Anonymous, quoted in Bobbie Riggs, Court Hustler, 1973

Resort address:
34567 Cathedral Canyon Dr.
Palm Springs, CA. 92264
Phone: (619)321-9000
(800)824-8224
Fax: No
No of rooms: 162
Estimated rates: Seasonal
Business facilities: Yes
Concierge: No
Sports facilities: Tennis
Dancing: Yes
Baby-sitting: No

Course: Cathedral Canyon C.C.
Architect: David Rainville
Pro: J.B.Kemp
Statistics: 18-holes opened in 1974
Yardage/Rating/Slope
Back Tees: 6505/72.6/128
Middle tees: 6172/69.5/117
Front tees: 5346/70.8/113
Guest policy: Members & hotel guests
Dress code: Resort attire
Golf fees: Seasonal
Cart fees: Incl.
Carts on cart path only: No
Caddies: No
Guests carry bags: No
Guests pull carts: No
Golf packages: No
Pro-shop phone:
(619)328-6571

Location: Hwy.10, exit at Date Palm. Turn right on Ramon, and turn left on Cathedral Canyon Dr.

Desert Princess Resort

My first impression of this resort was one of wide open spaces. The golf course is encircled by lovely townhouses. A lot of thought was given to the their uniform architecture, which causes them to blend into the desert landscape better than any other resort complex in the desert area. The result is an unobstructed view of the mountains from all eighteen fairways.

The hotel is a four-story contemporary building, designed in concert with the two hundred surrounding townhouses. The atmosphere is luxurious: light marble floors enhance the Southwestern interior design of the public areas. The rooms are spacious, each with its own balcony.

The Desert Princess golf course appeals to the high and low handicap player. There are thirteen water holes, and a myriad of sand traps on each fairway; combined, these require thoughtful course management. The 15th hole, for example, is a dog-leg right with water also on the right side; a good player can either shorten the distance by playing to the right (therefore chancing a fishing trip), or follow the lead of the high handicap player and play down the middle, using a lesser club so as not to end up in the rough.

The 18th is the signature hole... tough, because of water on both sides of the narrow fairway... but also a very picturesque ending to a satisfying or frustrating round....

Word of caution: late afternoon breezes could make the course play a couple of strokes higher....

The resort is now building 9 additional holes. Completion date is expected to be May/June 1990.

In addition to an amazing golf course, the resort has ten tennis courts (5 lighted for night play), and a fully equipped fitness center with two indoor racquetball courts. Post-workout massage? Of course...

Resort address:
67-967 Vista Chino
Cathedral City, CA.92234
Phone: (619)322-7000
(800)637-0577
Fax: (619)322-6853
No. of rooms: 289
Estimated rates: Seasonal
Business facilities: Yes
Concierge: Yes
Sports facilities:
Tennis,exercise rooms, spa
Dancing: Yes
Baby-sitting: Yes

Course: Desert Princess
Architect: David Rainville
Pro: David McKeating
Statistics: 18-holes opened in 1985
Yardage/Rating/Slope
Back Tees: 6636/71.4/118
Middle tees: 5719/69.1/111
Front tees: 5326/69.9/119
Guest policy: Members and resort guests
Dress code: Resort attire
Golf fees:
Weekdays $50
Weekends $60
Cart fees: Included
Carts on cart path only: No
Caddies: No
Guests carry bags: No
Guests pull carts: No
Golf packages: Yes, seasonal
Pro-shop phone:
(619)322-2280

Location: Hwy. 10 exit on Date Palm to Vista Chino.

Hyatt Grand Champions Resort

The Moorish architecture, in a desert setting with the rugged San Jacinto mountains in the background, invites guests to fulfill their vacation fantasies in an ambience combining European elegance with the casual California lifestyle.

Afternoon tea is served each day at the Regency Club. Guests are personally escorted there by the Concierge between 2 and 4 PM to enjoy tea served in the tradition of England's finest tea rooms.

Twenty garden villas feature courtyards and private jaccuzis, luxuriously and tastefully designed, each contains a living room, dining room and two bedrooms. Villas are staffed by British-trained butlers.

Located in the center of Indian Wells, this resort offers golf at two 18-hole championship courses adjoining the resort's property.

The East and West courses are equally challenging; between them there are 16 water holes, multi-tiered greens, and elevated tees up to 60 feet and several up and down hill lies.

The 13th hole on the East Course, is a par 4, island fairway surrounded by water. One's tee shot has to clear the widest part of the lake and supposedly land on tho island fairway. If you over shoot, slice or hook ... well, it's fishing time... then more water to cross before hitting on to the groen.

The West Course has a mean"dog leg" right on the 16th that has to clear water on the right side and in front of the green. I believe this is their "signature hole."

HGC has a 10,500 seat tennis stadium, home of the Newsweek Champions Cup. The tennis courts include eight hard, two clay and two grass... several are lighted for night play.

...continued on page 117

Resort address:
44-600 Indian Wells Lane
Indian Wells, CA. 92210
Phone: (619)341-1000
(800)826-1112 CA.
(800)233-1234 Nationwide
FAX: (619)568-2238
No. of rooms: 334
Estimated rates: Seasonal
Baby-sitting: Yes
Concierge: Yes
Business facilities: Yes
Sports facilities: Tennis, pools, Spa
Dancing: Yes

Course: Indian Wells East and West Courses, opened in 1986
Architect: Ted Robinson
Pro: Ron Cleveland
Yardage/Rating/Slope
East Course:
Back Tees: 6686/71.3/118
Middle tees: 6259/69.4/110
Front tees: 5521/70.7/113
West Course:
Back Tees: 6478/70.3/116
Middle tees: 6115/68.7/109
Front tees: 5387/70.0/111
Guest policy: Resort guests and public
Dress code: Resort attire
Golf fees: Seasonal
Cart fees: Incl.
Carts on cart path only: No
Caddies: No
Guests carry bags: No
Guests pull carts: No
Golf packages: Yes
Pro-shop phone:
(619)346-GOLF

Location: Off of Hwy.111

Industry Hills and Sheraton Resort

The Babe Zaharias Course and the adjacent Eisenhower Course are two of the best public courses in California. Both courses are very tough and are definitely no place for the beginner, the "Ike" is a long course with wide fairways lined with high rough and plenty of hills.

Although walking is permitted, I think that walking this course would be sheer madness. The entire course sits high above the City of Industry, offering a spectacular view of the mountains, (smog permitting). The second hole is a par 4, with an elevated tee 100 feet above the green. The waterfall next to the green collects it's share of balls...

The "Babe" is not as long as the "Ike", but is a very difficult course requiring very straight shots on most fairways. High rough, water, hilly fairways, rocks, bunkers, make for a frustrating game.

To return to the parking lot, you'll ride the only golf cart funicular in the world.

Although these are public golf courses, it is almost impossible to get a starting time for a weekend game unless one is a guest at the Sheraton Hotel, situated on the grounds of the golf course.

The Ralph Miller Golf Library is located on the second level of the Hotel. Enthusiasts can find quite a bit of golf memorabilia and museum items on display, such as Bobby Jones' irons and President Ford's putter.

> ***"When I win the lottery, I'm going to pay somebody to play this game (golf) for me."***
> — Ike Masey

Resort address:
One Industry Hills Parkway
City of Industry, CA. 91744
Phone: (818)965-0861
(800)325-3535
FAX: (818)964-9535
No. of rooms: 296
Estimated rates: From $105 to $225
Business facilities: Yes
Sports facilities: Tennis, pool & spa
Dancing: Yes

Courses:
The "Babe" 18-holes, opened in1980
The "Ike" 18-holes, opened in 1979
Designer: William Bell
Pro: Rick Smith
Yardage/Rating/Slope
The Babe:
Back-Tees: 6735/74.2/144
Middle-tees: 6519/72.9/137
Front-tees: 6132/70.3/130
The Eisenhower:
Back-Tees: 7192/76.6/149
Middle-tees: 6704/73.5/138
Front-tees: 6270/70.9/130
Guests policy: Public
Dress code: C.C.
Golf fees: $40 Weekdays: $45 Weekends: $55
Cart fees: Included
Carts on cart path only: Yes
Caddies: No
Guests carry bags: Yes
Guests pull carts: No
Golf packages: Yes
Pro-shop phone:
(818)810-GOLF

...continued on page 117

La Costa Hotel & Spa

La Costa is the vacation experience for the discriminating golfer desiring the ultimate in self indulgence.

The lounge and surroundings are really quite lovely. The rooms are spacious and very strikingly decorated and appointed with all the comforts of home. And what isn't there... ask and you shall receive....

For the past 18 years La Costa has hosted the MONY Tournament of Champions, played 9-holes on the South Course and 9-holes on the North Course. Tournament pros have labeled its last four holes "the longest mile", not because of the length of the holes, but because of the strong head winds coming off the ocean.

The North Course is also challenging. The 16th, a par 3, plays a lake from the left heading to an undulated green surrounded by bunkers and backed by a waterfall. The South Course's 17th hole is a true test of driving skill, the following fairway shots must also be well thought out in this hole. Both courses are worthy of play.

La Costa Spa is world renowned. Entertainment celebrities, corporate executives and foreign dignitaries who have been guests at La Costa return often to enjoy the extensive luxuries of the Spa. Relax in a sauna, rock steam bath, Roman pool, or Swiss shower, and schedule yourself for a facial, herbal wrap, massage or loofah scrub.

Now, let's talk about the food. There are seven restaurants including the special Spa Dining Room where the calorie-conscious guest feels as if every meal is a celebration of life. Then there are the Champagne Room, Cafe Figaro, The Gaucho Steak House, Pisces, Joe Wong and Brasserie La Costa. To properly describe the ambience and the wonderful food of each restaurant would require a booklet of its own. So, you must do your own research or try each one. You'll not be disappointed.

Tennis is played on hard, clay and lawn courts.

La Costa is truly a self sufficient resort. First-run movies are shown nightly to guests; several gift shops and very well-stocked golf and tennis shops are open daily.

Resort address:
Costa Del Mar
Carlsbad, CA. 92009
Phone: (619)438-9111
(800)854-5000
FAX: (619)438-3758
No. of rooms: 482
Estimated rates: From $210 to $350
Business facilities: Yes
Sports facilities: Tennis, spas, fitness programs
Dancing: Yes

Courses: North and South opened in 1960
Architect: Dick Wilson
Pro: Jack Millard
Yardage/Rating/Slope
North Course:
Back Tees: 6983/74.2/133
Middle tees: 6596/71.8/125
Front tees: 5980/74.0/127
South Course:
Back Tees: 6896/73.7/133
Middle tees: 6534/71.5/128
Front tees: 5632/72.1/123
Guest policy: Resort Guest and Members only
Dress code: Resort attire
Golf fees: $60
Cart fees: $25
Carts on cart path only: Yes
Caddies: Yes
Guests carry bags: No
Guests pull carts: No
Golf packages: Yes
Pro-shop phone:
(619)438-9111, ext.4243

Location: I-5, exit at La Costa Ave. off-ramp East, then left to Costa Del Mar Rd.

La Quinta Hotel

La Quinta opened in 1926, immediately becoming the favorite hideaway for "Hollywood's Golden Era," and the site of the first golf course in the Coachella Valley. La Quinta served as the inspiration for Frank Capra's "It Happened One Night". Today, the hotel remains the choice destination for discriminating celebrities, business leaders and sports notables.

Spanish dictionaries give "La Quinta" a variety of meanings: "Fifth Day," the day of rest following four days of exhausting travel between settlements and missions when California was Spanish and Mexican; or "A Special Place" or "Country Villa." Whichever you prefer, you'll find this resort to be serene, elegant, warm and relaxing.

The cuisine is excellent in any of the diverse restaurants. La Mirage is ideal for intimate, romantic dinners. The Morgans is a Cafe where the chef creates "Blue Plate Specials", like those served in the 20's. The Adobe Grill serves Mexican Cuisine with style and flair. High Tea is served in the Lounge every afternoon.

Many suites and guest rooms have wood burning fireplaces, a romantic touch on cool desert nights; others have private spas and pools. Whichever you choose, you'll find the rooms spacious and the decor reminiscent of the 20's (with all the updated comforts).

The Tennis Club offers guests several tennis courts with different surfaces: hard, grass and clay.

Pete Dye designed the Dunes and Citrus Courses. The Dunes'17th hole was named by Golf Digest as the toughest hole in the USA. From the championship tees the course plays to 6300 yards only, but seems a lot longer, perhaps because of tight play and doglegs, plus a lot of water and sand. "The Citrus" is 2 miles away from the hotel and may be played by guests after 11:00 AM. The course is relatively flat, with orange tree orchards bordering several holes. The signature holes are nos.6,13 and 18. No.13, par 3, plays 145 yds over water with bunkers right and left of the green.

Resort address:
44-499 Eisenhower Dr.
La Quinta, CA. 92253
Phone: (619)564-4111
(800)472-4316 in CA.
(800)854-1271 Nationwide
FAX: (619)564-5758
No. of rooms: 640
Estimated rates:
Rooms: $80 to $260
Suites: $360 to $1,800
Business facilities: Yes
Sports facilities: Tennis & pools
Dancing: Yes
Dunes, opened in 1978
Pro: Joye Pickauance
Citrus, opened in 1985.
Pro: Rick Neal
Designer for both courses:
Pete Dye
Yardage/Rating/Slope
Dunes:
Back Tees: 6300/70.6/139
Middle tees: 5798/67/124
Front tees: 5024/67.9/107
Citrus:
Back Tees: 6477/70.9/123
Middle tees: 5932/68.0/110
Front tees: 5106/68.3/112
Guest policy: Hotel guests and members only
Dress code: Country club attire
Golf fees: Dunes and Citrus:$75
Cart fees: Included
Carts on cart path only: Yes
Caddies: No
Guests carry bags: No
Guests pull carts: No
Golf packages: Yes
Pro-shop phone:
Dunes: (619)345-2549
Citrus: (619)564-7620

...continued on page 117

Lawrence Welk Resort

It all began 25 years ago as four-room motel with a modest restaurant, bordering a nine hole golf course. Lawrence Welk's "little bit of heaven on earth" has since developed into a 134-room destination resort.

The original nine-hole course is now an 18-hole executive course nicknamed the

Monster. Twisting slopes, centuries old oak trees and four lakes strategically located through the golf course are there to dispel the notion that this is "just another little executive course."

In addition to the Monster, there is the super-challenging 6,500 yard Meadow Lake Golf Course, just five minutes away.

This is a self-contained resort, with shops, nightly entertainment, a theater, beauty shop and even medical facilities. Multiple other recreational facilities include tennis, swimming pools and lovely picnic areas.

For those who cannot leave business behind, there are fully appointed meeting and conference rooms, sequestered at the edge of a fairway.

"For the first two or three days after I won, I kept calling the number where you can get your bank balance, and listened to it over and over again."
— Leonard Thompson, after winning $180,000 at the Buick Open

Address:
8860 Lawrence Welk Dr.
Escondido, CA. 92026
Phone: (619)749-3000
(800)932-9355
Fax: (619)749-6182
No. of rooms: 132
Estimated rates: From $80 to $220
Business facilities: Yes
Concierge: No
Sports facilities: Tennis & pool
Dancing: Yes
Course: Fountains and Meadow Lake
Architect: David Rainville
Fountains:
Pro: Randy C. Olson
Course: Meadow Lake
Pro: Jim Gilbert
Statistics:
Fountains: Executive, built in 1986
Yardage/Rating/Slope
Fountains:
Back Tees: 4002/57.3/95
Middle tees: 3581/54.6/89
Front tees: 3099/58.1/84
Meadow Lake: built in 1965
Back tees: 6521/72.5/131
Middle tees: 6312/71.0/124
Front tees: 5758/72.8/123
Guest policy: Resort guests & public
Dress code: Resort attire
Golf fees:
Fountains,
Weekdays $16
Weekends $20
Meadow Lake,
Weekdays $30
Weekends $34

...continued on page 118

Marriott's Desert's Springs and Resort

Terraced waterfalls and a curving lagoon within a soaring 8-story lobby set the pace for other surprises to come, such as five fine restaurants and three lounges, one with dancing every night. An "African Queen" type boat will take you on a tour of the lakes during the day, and at night taxi you to two of the resort restaurants.

The rooms are luxurious, with balconies or patios. Gorgeous views.

There are not one, but two championship golf courses: the Palms and The Valley. Both are wonderful examples which show that Ted Robinson, "king of waterscapes" outdid himself on these two courses. The Palms has 13, holes with lakes and waterfalls crossing the fairways. The 17th hole, a par 3, 160 yds, has an island green. To reach the green your shot must carry over a water-fall to a well bunkered green. The green also has a small strip of palm trees and sand traps. The rest is all water... The Valley course has 11 water holes and is found to be quite demanding, with small landing areas off the tee and equally challenging greens. The Valley course is rated as the tougher of the two courses. Golf Digest nominated The Valley as one of the best new resort courses of 1988.

Both courses have fairways with beautifully manicured Bermuda grass and undulating two and three-tier greens. Ted Robinson also designed an 18-hole, par 54 putting course with easy access from the main lobby. This is truly "golf in miniature," and very popular with the young set.

Another surprise is the 12,000 sq. ft. white sandy beach. Other features include tennis (the courts...3 of them clay...are night lighted), boccie ball, badminton,volleyball, a driving range, and a full luxurious spa. Specialty shops and beauty services round out your experience at this activity filled resort.

Resort address:
74855 Country Club Dr.
Palm Desert, CA. 92260
Phone: (619)341-2211
(800)228-9290
Fax: (619)341-1730
No. of rooms: 891
Estimated rates: Seasonal
Business facilities: Yes
Concierge: Yes
Sports facilities: Tennis, pools, boccie ball, badminton, volleyball, spa.
Dancing: Yes
Baby-sitting: Yes

Course: The Palm and The Valley opened in 1986
Architect: Ted Robinson
Pro: Tim Skogen
Statistics: 18-holes each
Yardage/Rating/Slope
The Palm:
Front Tees: 6143/69.0/114
Back tees: 6761/72.0/124
Middle tees: 6381/70.2/118
The Valley:
Front Tees: 6679/72.1/124
Back tees: 6377/70.4/121
Middle tees: 6063/68.5/109
Guest policy: Resort Guests
Dress code: Resort attire
Golf fees: $85
Cart fees: Incl.
Carts on cart path only: Yes
Caddies: No
Guests carry bags: No
Guests pull carts: No
Golf packages: Several
Pro-shop phone:
(619)341-2211

Location: On I-10 exit on Country Club Dr.

Pala Mesa Resort

Golf at Pala Mesa is outstanding. Fresh morning air and cool afternoon breezes enhance one of California's most challenging and beautiful championship courses. The fairways are narrow and lined with stately sycamore, oak and pine trees. There are several elevated tees and greens. Every hole is a challenge. No.1 seems benign, but wait until after you tee off....

All guests rooms have now been refurbished. They are spacious, airy and very comfortable.

The restaurant overlooks the 1st tee... that's entertainment! Let's not forget the well prepared and well presented food. J.P.'s the friendly lounge with lively dancing music in the evenings. The attire is resort casual.

There are tennis courts and a swimming pool, a driving range and a pitching green in addition to the putting green.

Pala Mesa is a challenging golf course that requires player concentration and a fair knowledge of course management before each shot is played. A good game will bring you back time after time...

"I didn't realize how preoccupied I had become with golf until I went to church, the minister said, 'Let us pray,' I clasped my hands and it was an interlocking grip."
— Anonymous, from *2400 Jokes to Brighten Your Speeches*, by Robert Orben

Resort address:
2001 Old Hwy. 395
Fallbrook, CA. 92028
Phone: (619)728-5881
(800)722-4700 CA.
(800)822-4600 outside CA.
FAX: (619)723-8292
No. of rooms: 133
Estimated rates: From $95 to $180
Business facilities: Yes
Sports facilities: Tennis
Dancing: Yes
Baby-sitting: No

Course: Pala Mesa
Designer: Dick Ross
Pro: Chris Starkjohann
Statistics: 18-holes built in 1960
Yardage/Rating/Slope
Back Tees: 6472/71.1/123
Middle tees: 6151/69.5/117
Front tees: 5814/73.0/123
Guest policy: Resort Guests and Public
Dress code: Resort attire
Golf fees:
Weekdays:$45
Weekends $50
Cart fees: Incl.
Carts on cart path only: No
Caddies: No
Guests carry bags: No
Guests pull carts: No
Golf packages: Yes
Pro-shop phone:
(619) 728-5881

Location: Hwy.15, exit on Hwy.76 and turn right on Old Hwy.395

Quails Inn at Lake San Marcos

The guests at the Quails Inn can enjoy a very active outdoor life in the atmosphere of casual charm and serenity.

The 18-hole championship golf course plus an executive 18-hole course will satisfy the most ardent golfers. A few steps from your room are the regulation tennis and paddle tennis courts.

After golf, enjoy a leasure sail around the resort's 1 1/3 mile-long lake. Don't like sailing? How about taking one of the resort's rowboats, canoes or Kayot party boats while enjoying a cool drink? Or just lie by one of the four swimming pools and soak up the sun. The resort boasts an average of 340 clear warm days a year, so there's not much chance of being "rained out."

> ***"Golf is not, on the whole, a game for realists. By it's exactitudes of measurement has invited the attention of perfectionists."***
>
> — Heywood Hale Broun

Resort address:
1025 La Bonita Dr.
San Marcos, CA. 92069
Phone: (619)744-0120
Fax: (619)744-0748
No. of rooms: 142
Estimated rates: From $80 to $200
Services: Airport pick-up
Business facilities: Yes
Concierge: No
Sports facilities: Tennis, and paddle tennis, sailing, rowing and swimming
Dancing: Yes

Course: Lake San Marcos C.C.
Architect: Gordon Frazar
Pro: Bob Hitzel
Statistics: 18-holes opened in 1962
Yardage/Rating/Slope
Back Tees: 6484/70.2/116
Middle tees: 6260/69.2/110
Front tees: 5959/74.1/117
Guest policy: Members & resort guests
Dress code: Resort attire
Golf fees: $40
Cart fees: Included
Carts on cart path only: No
Caddies: No
Guests carry bags: No
Guests pull carts: No
Golf packages: Yes
Pro-shop phone:
(619)744-1310

Directions: From I-15, take the Hwy.78 off-ramp to San Marcos Blvd. exit. Left to Rancho Santa Fe Rd..Or from I-5, exit East on Palomar Airport Rd.. Right to Rancho Santa Fe Rd.

Rancho Las Palmas

Hospitality, California style...warm, inviting. Picturesque two-story haciendas with white stucco walls and red tile roofs house 456 spacious guest rooms and suites, decorated in warm terra cotta tones. Each has its own veranda overlooking fairways and lakes where ducks swim freely.

There are three nine hole courses. The North, South and West courses are scenic and offer the Resort guest a few challenges. Keep in mind that this course was designed for the enjoyment of the high and low-handicap player. The greens are slightly undulated. The 27 hole course is short but sporty. Six lakes and sharp doglegs demand an accurate game.

Rancho Las Palmas has 25 tennis courts (eight lighted for night play), and three clay courts. For tournament play there is a 1,000 seat stadium court. There are three swimming pools, an exercise room and two whirlpools.

This resort is owned and operated by Marriott hotels, so you can trust the restaurants to be up to Marriott standards, Rancho Las Palmas offers four theme restaurants and an after-hours Cantina with music and dancing every night.

> ***"Playing golf is a little like carving a turkey. It helps if you have your slice under control."***
>
> — Anonymous, from *2400 Jokes to Brighten Your Speeches*, by Robert Orben

Resort address:
4100 Bob Hope Dr.
Rancho Mirage, CA. 92270
Phone: (619)568-2727
(800)458-8786
Fax: (619)568-5845
No. of rooms: 450
Estimated rates: From $99 to $260
Business facilities: None
Sports facilities: Tennis & pool
Dancing: Yes
Restrictions: No pets

Course: Rancho Las Palmas Country Club
Designer: Ted Robinson
Pro: Ray Metz
Statistics: 27 holes, opened in 1979
Yardage/Rating/Slope:
North/South:
Back Tees: 6019/67.2/115
Middle tees: 5716/65.7/103
Front tees: 5421/69.7/113
North/West:
Back Tees: 5558/65.3/105
Middle tees: 5295/63.7/100
Front tees: 4985/66.9/105
South/West:
Back Tees: 5569/65.6/106
Middle tees: 5219/63.9/97
Front tees: 4885/66.8/110
Guest policy: Resort Guests and members
Dress code: Resort attire
Golf fees: $67 (seasonal)
Cart fees: Included
Carts on cart path only: No
Caddies: No
Guests carry bags: No
Guests pull carts: No
Golf packages: Yes, several

...continued on page 118

Rancho Bernardo Inn

This is one of my favorite resorts in California. Located in the San Bernardo Valley and surrounded by the San Pasqual Mountains, Rancho Bernardo has an ambience unlike any other resort I have visited.

The moment you enter the Inn's lobby, you'll feel welcome at this warm and elegant country resort. Exquisite antiques and furnishings convey a sense honest hospitality.

High Tea is served every afternoon in the Music Room to the soothing sound of a piano playing your favorite classics. There are two excellent restaurants. The Veranda, for breakfast and lunch, is bright and cheerful. El Bizcocho for dinner is quite elegant. The menu is French, the wine cellar stores over 350 premier wines, and after a superlative dessert, you'll want to walk to La Bodega lounge for entertainment and dancing.

Golf at Rancho Bernardo is surprisingly deceptive. The last hole is a tough home stretch. Par 5, tee shot, is from an elevated green that has to be well placed for a straight shot to the also elevated green over a large drainage ditch. Then your 3rd shot should put you on the green... if you miss the cascading water coming off the lake in front of the green. If you overshoot the green, you'll be on the road, the putting green, or the coffee shop.

Christmas is a festive and merry event at the Inn. The staff is attired in Dickensian costumes. A cocktail party is hosted by the Inn on Christmas Eve, when you'll be entertained by the Raggle Taggle Players, well known for their interpretation of the Dickens' Christmas masterpiece, a Christmas Carol. There are several activities planned for children ages 4-17 under the constant supervision of the staff of the Inn's Holiday Camp.

In addition to a challenging par 72 golf course, there are other recreational facilities: 12 tennis courts (4 night lighted), 2 outdoor pools, 5 jacuzzis,

...continued on page 118

Resort address:
17550 Bernardo Oaks Drive
San Diego, CA. 2128
Phone: (619)487-1611
(800)542-6096 in CA.
(800)854-1067 outside Ca.
Fax: (619)673-0311
No. of rooms: 287
Estimated rates: From $115 to $185
Services: Limousine to and from airport
Business facilities: Yes
Sports facilities:
Tennis, Spa, Fitness Center and Swimming pools
Dancing: Yes
Baby-sitting: Yes

Course: Rancho Bernardo, built in 1965
Designer: William Bell
Pro: Tom Wilson
Yardage/Rating/Slope
Back Tees: 3161/70.2/116
Middle tees: 3034/69.1/112
Front tees: 2691/71.0/117
Guest policy: Resort guests, members and public
Dress code: Resort attire
Golf fees: $40
Cart fees: Included
Carts on cart path only: No
Caddies: No
Guests carry bags: Yes
Guests pull carts: Yes
Golf packages: Yes
Pro-shop phone:
(619)487-0700

Location: Hwy.15, exit on Rancho Bernardo Rd. and turn East to Bernardo Oaks Dr.

The Ritz-Carlton Resort Hotel

Ernest Hemingway once said that he pictured his afterlife taking place at the Ritz. The Ritz-Carlton at Laguna Niguel lives up to the lovely tradition of the Ritz of the Hemingway years.

The hotel rests on a 150-foot bluff overlooking the ocean...a short walk to the Links at Monarch Beach. Everything from the marble and silk-lined lobby to the 393 guest rooms is superbly appointed. The resort is steward to one of the finest art collections. Antique English and Russian crystal chandeliers light the muted Jeffersonian color scheme. Antique navigational tools, priceless marine portraits and antique books are to be enjoyed by guests having their afternoon high tea.

There are two swimming pools, four tennis courts, volleyball and two miles of sandy beach to be enjoyed by the non golfer or to be used apres-golf before it's time to enjoy a superb gourmet dinner.

The Links is designed almost entirely in the Scottish tradition, following the coastline or set-up along side of a creek. The undulating greens and gathering bunkers are Non-Scottish features. Quite a bit of water comes into play on seven fairways. No.3, par 3 green, is flanked by water on three sides with a big bunker in front. The elevated tee and prevailing winds cause this hole to play shorter, but require a straight shot off the tee.

"Perfect retirement: To live in a house by the side of a golf course, and have your best friend be a doctor."

— Anonymous

Resort address:
33533 Ritz Carlton Dr.
Dana Point, CA. 92677
Phone: (714)240-2000
Fax: (714)240-0829
No. of rooms: 393
Estimated rates: From $185 to $400
Business facilities: Yes
Sports Facilities: Tennis, volleyball, badminton and swimming
Dancing: Yes

Course: The Links at Monarch Beach
Designer: Robert Trent Jones Jr.
Pro: Mike Mumper
Statistics: 18-holes opened in 1987
Yardage/Rating/Slope:
Back Tees: 6243/70.0/127
Middle tees: 5655/67.0/117
Front tees: 4984/N.A/N.A
Guest policy: Resort guests and Public
Dress code: Resort attire
Golf fees:
Weekdays: $50
Weekends: $75
Cart fees: Included
Carts on cart path only: No
Caddies: Yes
Guests carry bags: No
Guests pull carts: No
Golf packages: No
Pro-shop phone:
(714)240-8247

Location: From the I-5 take Crown Valley Parkway exit west to Pacific Coast Hwy. Then procced south one mile to Ritz-Carlton Dr.

Singing Hills Country Club And Lodge

Three of California's most beautiful golf courses lie within this 720-acre resort in the El Cajon valley. A continuous breeze channeled between the mountains from the ocean keeps this resort smog-free, with crystal clear nights for viewing the galaxy that city people seldom can enjoy in Southern California.

Two courses... Oak Glen and Willow Glen... are superb championship courses. The third, Pine Glen, is a charming par-3 course.

Willow Glen is the tougher of the two courses. I definitely do not suggest walking this course. The walk from no. 3 green to no. 4 tee is straight uphill.... where you are rewarded with an impossible par 4, #3 handicap hole over a ravine and, for your second shot, a lake approximately 100 yds in front of the green surrounded by glistening white sand traps. There are other tough holes .... An "ex-river" which is now a giant sand bunker runs along several fairways.

Oak Glen is kinder, and a good walking course. But don't think this course is a push over. It affords plenty of challenges, such as a par three with a lake in front of the green, instead of fairway, surrounded by big oak trees and of course... sand traps. There are many other challenging holes, but I'll not spoil the surprises that will be unfolded by telling you any more than I have already.

Both courses have spotlessly manicured greens and fairways lined with old oak, willow and olive trees, and the tee boxes are backed by seasonal flowers.

Singing Hills, being a semi-private course, alternates the two courses between members and lodge guests, giving you the opportunity to play both courses.

All of the Lodge's rooms are situated around the golf course in small two-story buildings. Guests usually gather on the putting greens by their rooms with their drinks for putting contests at sundown.

...continued on page 118

Resort address:
3007 Dehesa Rd.
El Cajon, CA. 92021
Phone: (619)422-3425
Fax: (619)442-9575
No. of rooms: 102
Estimated rates: From $70 to $200
Business facilities: Yes
Concierge: No
Sports facilities: Tennis
Dancing: Yes
Baby-sitting: No

Courses: Oak Glen, Willow Glen and Pine Glen
Architect: Ted Robinson
Pro: Tom Addis,III
Statistics: 18-holes each, opened in 1980
Yardage/Rating/Slope
Oak Glen
Back Tees: 6138/69.0/
Middle tees: 5749/67.0
Front tees: 5308/69.3/112
Willow Glen:
Back Tees: 6608/71.5/
Middle tees: 6247/68.9/
Front tees: 5585/71.4/119
Guest policy: Members,resort guests & public
Dress code: Resort attire
Golf fees:
Weekdays $20
Weekends $25
Cart fees: $17
Carts on cart path only: No
Caddies: No
Guests carry bags: Yes
Guests pull carts: Yes
Golf packages: Yes
Pro-shop phone:
(619)442-3425

...continued on page 118

San Luis Rey Downs Golf and Tennis Resort

Hidden away in the relaxed country atmosphere of the San Luis Rey Valley, this mature course has the distinction of being one of San Diego County's oldest and most respected public golf courses.

The "Downs" is known for its demanding par 3's (five in all) and fairways that are lined by large trees. The 16th, a par 3, is feared by all players regardless of handicap. To par this hole one needs a very straight drive into the wind and two putts only, which is not easy on this green....A bogey is a respectable score.

Several beautiful water holes (nos. 5, 9 and 10) add to the charm, character and challenge enjoyed by all levels of golfers at the "Downs".

In addition, the resort has four tennis courts, all night lighted, and a lovely garden setting framing the swimming pool area.

The lodge offers rest and tranquillity. There are only 28 spacious guest-rooms, and they have private patios overlooking the 7th, 8th and 9th fairways. This "little gem" has been a well kept secret. Up to now anyway...

"I play my best golf when I leave my ego in the Club House. Then, I can be kind to myself."

— Anonymous

Resort address:
31474 Golf Club Dr.
Bonsall, CA. 92003
Phone: (619)758-3762
No. of rooms: 28
Estimated rates: From $65 to $85
Business facilities: Yes
Concierge: No
Sports facilities: Tennis, swimming, equestrian
Dancing: Yes
Baby-sitting: No

Course: San Luis Rey Downs
Architect: Billy Bell
Pro: "Pinky" Stevenson
Statistics: 18-holes built in 1960
Yardage/Rating/Slope
Back Tees: 6610/71.2/118
Middle tees: 6324/69.6/111
Front tees: 5547/71.4/118
Guest policy: Resort guests & public
Dress code: Golf attire
Golf fees:
Weekdays $20
Weekends $28
Cart fees: $16
Carts on cart path only: No
Caddies: No
Guests carry bags: Yes, weekdays only
Guests pull carts: Yes, as above
Golf packages: Yes
Pro-shop phone:
(619)758-9699

Location: Hwy.15, exit on Camino Del Rey and turn left on Golf Club Dr.

Stouffer Esmeralda Resort

Once upon a time when the Spanish "entered" the Inca capital in Peru. Los Indios spoke of a fabulous green stone set in the forehead of the Inca sun god; its green fire lighted the entire room. In awe, the Conquistador uttered one word: "Esmeralda"!

In due course the stone was taken to Spain and cut into exquisite jewels, and a necklace of fabulous beauty was created. And from then on the necklace was known as Esmerada. The story goes on...and one day a famous jeweler designed the Legend of Esmeralda necklace, now on display at the Resort. Worth $200,000, the necklace will eventually be given to a charitable cause.

The Esmeralda Resorts is within walking distance from the two championship golf courses: Indian Wells East and West.

The East and West courses are equally challenging, between them there are 16 water holes, multi-tiered greens, some tees are elevated 60 feet and lots of up and down hill lies.

The 13th hole on the East Course, is a par 4, island fairway surrounded by water. One's tee shot has to clear the widest part of the lake and supposedly land in the island fairway. If you over shoot, slice or hook ... well, it's fishing time... then more water to cross before hitting on to the green.

The West Course has a mean "dog leg" right on the 16th that has to clear water on the right side and in front of the green. I believe this is their "signature hole".

North African white ash is used throughout the public places. The guest rooms have balconies and Bermuda shutters.

The sound of water falling begins at the entrance and continues through the lobby where a stream feeds a series of waterfalls which welcomes you to the area's largest swimming pools. One of the three pools has a sandy beach.

Resort address:
44-400 Indian Wells Lane
Indian Wells, CA. 92210
Phone: (619)773-4444
(800)USA-MEET
FAX: (619)773-9250
No. of rooms: 560
Estimated rates: Seasonal
Baby-sitting: Yes
Concierge: Yes
Business facilities: Yes
Sports facilities: Tennis, pools, Spa
Dancing: Yes

Courses: Indian Wells East and West, built in 1986
Architect: Ted Robinson
Pro: Ron Cleveland
Yardage/Rating/Slope
East Course:
Back Tees: 6686/71.3/118
Middle tees: 6259/69.4/110
Front tees: 5521/70.7/113
West Course:
Back Tees: 6478/70.3/116
Middle tees: 6115/68.7/109
Front tees: 5387/70.0/111
Guest policy: Resort guests and public
Dress code: Resort attire
Golf fees: Seasonal
Cart fees: Incl.
Carts on cart path only: No
Caddies: Yes
Guests carry bags: No
Guests pull carts: No
Golf packages: Yes
Pro-shop phone:
(619)346- GOLF

Location: Hwy.111 turn into Indian Wells Lane.

Temecula Creek Inn

The Pechanga Indians used the word "Temecula" to describe the legendary light that appeared at dawn over the eastern mountain ranges and chased a ghostly mist from the valley floor.

Today, the same glowing aura rests over this remarkable resort.

Roses and other colorful flowers entwine the fences surrounding Temecula Creek Inn, creating a cheerful and welcome atmosphere.

The golf course has quite a few water hazards, white sand bunkers and rolling terrain surrounded by century old trees and roughs, where granite boulders still bear the marks of the ancient Pachanga.

This is a challenging, but not a discouraging course, where the low and the high handicap golfer can both have a very satisfying round. The 12th hole, par 4, should be played with the tee shot center left for a clear shot to the green, which cannot be seen until one arrives at the top of the hill. The lucky tee shot lands on a plateau (the only flat lie on this fairway); the faded or sliced shot can put your ball behind a tree or in the rough. The green is elevated and surrounded by a hill and sand traps, of course...

The entire ambience is Southwestern. All the rooms view the golf course or the distant San Jacinto mountains. The rooms are spacious, with balconies. Practical items such as safe deposit boxes and hair dryers are available in all rooms.

Consider making your dinner reservations when making your lodging arrangements because the restaurant is small and the Southwestern cuisine is wonderful! The attire is resort casual.

Temecula Creek is for golfers. But after golf, you'll find two tennis courts, an immaculate croquet green, a terrace pool with hydro-spa, and lovely walking trails. One of the trails leads to the Inn's historic "Stone House", built in the 1800's, and is now used for special functions such as authentic "buffalo barbecues."

An additional 9-hole course is now being built and should be ready for play by May 1990.

Resort address:
44501 Rainbow Canyon Rd.
Temecula, CA. 92390
Phone: (800)962-7335
(714)676-5631
Fax: (714)676-5631
No. of rooms: 80
Estimated rates: From $90 to $115
Business facilities: Yes
Concierge: No
Sports facilities: Tennis, croquet, swimming
Dancing: No

Course: Temecula Creek
Architect: Ted Robinson
Pro: Mike Bratschi
Yardage/Rating/Slope
Back Tees: 6782/72.6/125
Middle tees: 6375/69.8/111
Front tees: 5747/71.6/122
Guest policy: Resort guests and public
Dress code: Resort attire
Golf fees:
Weekday $19
Weekend $25
Cart fees: $18
Carts on cart path only: No
Caddies: No
Guests carry bags: Yes
Guests pull carts: Yes
Golf packages: Yes
Pro-shop phone:
(714)676-2405

Location: I-15, exit on Hwy.79 (to Palm Springs). 3/4 mile to Pala Rd., turn right to Rainbow Canyon Rd.

The Inn At Rancho Santa Fe

The Inn, built in 1923, was originally only meant to be a guest house for prospective land buyers. In 1941, George Richardson purchased the guest house and renamed it The Inn at Rancho Santa Fe. He then added many of the guest cottages and the beautiful gardens and walkways surrounding the property. Since 1958, the Inn has been owned and operated by the Stephen W. Royce family. The mission style architecture has been retained throughout the ranch, which has recently been redecorated, yet retains its Western old world charm.

Antique ship models and Oriental treasures belonging to the Royce family accessorise the main lounge, a very spacious room with a high rafted ceiling and a welcoming wood burning fire place.

There are three dining rooms. The Vintage Room, where guests dine and dance under the stars, is a replica of an old California taproom. The Garden Room overlooks the pool and surrounding gardens. The Library, the oldest of the three restaurants is lined with bookshelves flanking an always cheerfully burning fire place. The cuisine of all three restaurants is excellent. But don't neglect to explore the Village as well, and discover its charming and very good small restaurants.

The Inn maintains its own private cottage at the nearby Del Mar beach. Ask them to pack a picnic lunch for you.

Golf starting times are arranged by the concierge at the nearby Rancho Santa Fe Golf Course (Private), where the Inn has a membership for the use of its guests. This is a very challenging course and certainly worthy of praise for its immaculate upkeep.

Throughout the year the average daytime temperature is between 65° and 75°. At night, the temperature drops ten to twenty degrees. Great evening-dress-up weather...

Resort address:
Paseo Delicias
Rancho Santa Fe, CA. 92067
Phone: (619)756-1131
(800)654-2928
FAX: (619)759-1604
No. of rooms: 78
Estimated rates: From $90 to $175
Concierge: Yes
Business facilities: Yes
Sports facilities: Tennis
Dancing: No
Baby-sitting: No

Course: Rancho Santa Fe Country Club
Designer: Max Beahr
Pro: Chuck Courtney
Statistics: 18-holes built in 1928
Yardage/Rating/Slope
Back Tees: 6938/73.6/132
Middle tees: 6497/71.3/126
Front tees: 5950/73.8/123
Guest policy: Members and hotel guests
Dress code: Resort attire
Golf fees: $90
Cart fees: Incl.
Carts on cart path only: No
Caddies: No
Guests carry bags: No
Guests pull carts: No
Golf packages: None
Pro-shop phone:
(619)756-3094

Location: I-5, exit on Via De Lavalle (east) which merges into Paseo Delicias. The Inn is in the center of town.

Whispering Palms Resort

Whispering Palms is located in the heart of scenic Rancho Santa Fe, an elegant small community inhabited by those who love their serene and genteel country ways.

Whispering Palms, 27-hole golf course offers the visiting golfer a combination of three separate nines. The East Nine has recently been restructured, now playing to about 3400 yds; with additional water hazards and bunkers plus five new greens, the course is now more challenging.

As testament to the course's improvements, Whispering Palms was chosen as the site of the first Katherine Crosby/Honda LPGA Golf Classic and is also the home of the San Diego Golf Academy, which provides a two-year program for the development of future golf professionals.

Besides Golf, there are eleven championship tennis courts. The Village offers many boutiques and charming small restaurants with excellent food. The Del Mar race track is only two miles away.

The accommodations are simple, but the rooms are spacious, and many rooms overlook the golf course. All the public areas are now being remodeled in the Southwestern style; this is a fair improvement over the previous decor. The food is typically "country club". I strongly suggest exploring Rancho Santa Fe village after golf and making reservations for dinner at a restaurant of your choice.

Resort address:
4000 Cancha de Golf.
Rancho Santa Fe, CA. 92067
Phone: (619)756-2471
Fax: (619)756-3013
No. of rooms: 100
Estimated rates: From $68 to $132
Business facilities: Yes
Concierge: No
Sports facilities: Yes
Dancing: No
Baby-sitting: No

Course: Whispering Palms
Architect: Robert Raintree
Pro: John D.Combs
Statistics: 27-holes built in 1964
Yardage/Rating/Slope:
North/East
Back Tees: 6141/68.8/110
Middle tees: 5860/67.0/103
Front tees: 5564/70.2/113
East/ South
Back Tees: 6643/70.2/112
Middle tees: 6131/68.3/105
Front tees: 5776/71.3/117
South/North
Back tees: 6346/69.7/112
Midlle tees: 6051/67.9/105
Front tees: 5684/70.7/115
Guest policy: Members, resort-guests and public
Dress code: Resort attire
Golf fees:
Week days $20
Weekends $25
Cart fees: $20
Carts on cart path only: No
Caddies: No
Guests carry bags: Yes
Guests pull carts: Yes
Golf packages: Yes
Pro-shop phone:
(619)756-3255

San Vicente Country Club

San Vicente Resort is probably one of the most laid-back, unpretentious and friendly resorts in Southern California. Located in Ramona, north of San Diego, this resort is known for its great golf course. Everyone who has played it vows to return for another day of enjoyable golf or to conquer this lovely but difficult course.

The weather is mostly fair year round, but if rain should occur, then the big dry ditches that criss-cross the course fill with water and it would be reasonable to say that every hole has its water surprise. Even in dry weather, the course has its share of challenges. To mention just one: number 9 hole, requires a demanding tee shot because of a big oak tree in the middle of the fairway, where a driver would have to clear 230 yds. over this tree and stop dead not to end up in the ravine just beyond. It is preferable to hit a 2 iron and let it roll under the oak tree, stopping short of the ditch. Other fairways are narrow and require tee shots with accuracy. Terry Horn, the resort PGA golf pro, says he uses a 2 wood on number 5 for accuracy instead of a driver.

Frost occurs in the early mornings of the winter months, but seems to disappear by 9:00 AM. Shotgun starts seem to keep everything on schedule.

The resort facilities are unpretentious; recently the rooms have been refurbished. You'll find the people running the resort to be very friendly.

You'll be within an easy drive of the San Diego Wild Animal Park on the way to Escondido, which offers restaurants and lots of shopping locations.

The San Vicente Resort has a solar heated swimming pool, and several tennis courts.

Resort address:
24157 San Vicente Rd.
Ramona, CA. 92065
Phone: (619)789-8290
(800)765-7323
FAX: No
No. of rooms: 28
Reservation rates: With golf package only
Business facilities: Yes
Sports facilities: Tennis
Dancing: Yes
Baby-sitting: No

Course: San Vicente C.C.
Designer: Ted Robinson
Pro: Terry Horn
Statistics: 18-holes built in 1973
Yardage/Rating/Slope:
Back Tees: 6585/71.4/121
Middle tees: 6180/69.3/111
Front tees: 5578/71.2/124
Guest policy: Members and Resort guests
Dress code: Resort attire
Golf fees:
Weekdays $26
Weekends:$32
Cart fees: $16
Carts on cart path only: Yes
Caddies: No
Guests carry bags: No
Guests pull carts: No
Golf packages: Yes
Pro-shop phone:
(619)789-3477

Location: I-15 to S-4 exit which joins Hwy.67, follow the signs "to Ramona", turn off on San Vicente Rd., in the middle of the town of Ramona. Aprox. 6 miles to resort.

Carlton Oaks Country Club

This country club was literally reborn in 1989. Ten years ago, the kindest fate for this course would have been to put AstroTurf on the greens and let it go at that. Today, Carlton Oaks ranks as one of the best golf courses in Southern California.

Perry Dye and his team re-designed the entire course in the tradition of its patriarch, Pete Dye. The $4 million project took only ten months to complete. The removal of 350,000 cubic yards of earth produced the contours, sculptured mounds and terraces that give the players a sense of "privacy" rather than the big greenbelt sweep.

There are a few notable holes, such as No.11, with its dogleg around a lake playing into the wind. No.12, a par 3, has water surrounding the green on the right, a bunker on the left and only ten feet through which to thread your way to the green. Finally, No.18 is another dogleg into the wind, requiring an unerring approach shot, considering that a creek crosses in front of the green an a lake flanks it on the left.

This resort appeals to those looking for a weekend getaway offering a very reasonable golf package.

The ambience is very casual. The accommodations have all been remodeled and the restaurant is snug, boasting of the best food in the area. WARNING: there's nothing else in Santee.... I was impressed with the quality of the rental clubs: Ping golf clubs....

Resort address:
9200 Innwood Dr.
Santee, CA. 92071
Phone: (619)448-4242
Fax: (619)258-8736
No. of rooms:60
Estimated rates: From $63 to $163
Business facilities: Yes
Concierge: No
Sports facilities: Swimming
Dancing: No
Baby-sitting: No

Course: Carlton Oaks
Architect: Perry Dye
Pro: Rex Cole
Statistics: 18-holes re-opened in 1989
Yardage/Rating/Slope
Back Tees: 7109/73.2/143
Middle tees: 6084/69.0/117
Front tees: 5772/72.2/128
Guest policy: Resort guests & public
Dress code: Resort attire
Golf fees: $55
Cart fees: Included
Carts on cart path only: Yes
Caddies: No
Guests carry bags: No
Guests pull carts: No
Golf packages: Yes
Pro-shop phone:
(619)448-8500

Location: I-8 to the Hwy 67 North then turn left on Mission Gorge Rd. to Carlton Hills Blvd. and left on Carlton Oaks Dr.

Rancho California Golf Course

This is a most challenging public course with breathtaking views of the Temecula Valley from most fairways, which are steep and undulating. Frankly, I can't remember having a flat lie on the entire course.

Robert Sherwood, one of the golf professionals at Rancho California, considers No.12, par 4, to be the most challenging hole of this course: "water gets into play from the tee shot and again on the approach shot; a dog-leg left configuration and double tiered green surrounded by sand-traps make this an unforgettable hole."

Rancho California is adjacent to the old Murrieta Hot Springs Resort. In its day the Resort must have been very charming. Today, it is in dire need of total renovation; therefore I have chosen not to list it in this book as one of California's golf resorts.

However, the course itself was designed by Robert Trent Jones Senior in 1975 and, after being shut down for three years, was renovated by the same architect in 1988 and is now one of the "notable public golf courses" of California.

Rancho California is a "must play" course in the North County area. Ask the Pro at the resort of your choice to arrange starting times for you at Rancho California, and I promise you'll not be disappointed.

Course address:
38275 Murietta Hot
Springs Road
Murrieta, CA. 92362
Phone: (714)677-7446
Designer: Robert Trent Jones Senior
Pro: Wayne Hudson
Statistics: 18 holes built in 1975
Yardage/Rating/Slope
Back Tees: 7105/74.4/136
Middle tees: 6593/74.7/125
Front tees: 5426/68.8/116
Guest policy: Public
Dress code: Golf attire
Golf fees:
Week days: $30
Weekends: $45
Cart fees: Included
Carts on cart path only: No
Caddies: No
Guests carry bags: No
Guests pull carts: No

Location: Hwy.15, exit on Winchester Rd. and turn left on Murietta Hot Springs Rd.

Torrey Pines Municipal Golf Course

I can't imagine a golfer visiting San Diego and not playing at least one of the two Torrey Pines courses. The North or the South. It's not easy to get starting times at either of the courses, but if you call seven days in advance, the odds are that you'll get your starting time.

Torrey Pines is truly a golfer's paradise. Constrained by mountains to the north and the ocean to the west, these seaside courses are often swept by fog, rain and chilling winds. These challenging conditions contribute to the courses' reputation for some of golf's most thrilling final-day finishes on tournaments held there. The fair weather golfer should play in the summertime.

The South course's No. 1 handicap hole is No.4, a par 5. The cliff on the left and bunkers to the right plus the wind off the ocean justify this being the toughest hole in the course. The wind and a very small green make No. 8, a par 4, the most difficult hole of the North course. Both courses were designed for the enjoyment of "good" golfers.

Course address:
11480 North Torrey Pines Rd.
San Diego, CA. 92037
Phone: (619)453-0380
Courses: North and South
Architect: Billy Bell
Pro: Orin Vincent
Statistics:
North Course: 18-holes opened in 1956
Yardage/Rating/Slope
Back Tees: 6659/71.3 /144
Middle tees: 6375/69.6/116
Front tees: 6104/73.5/109
Statistics:
South Course: 18-holes opened in 1956
Yardage/Rating/Slope
Back Tees: 7021/74.0 /131
Middle tees: 6706/72.2/124
Front tees: 6447/75.8/114
Guest policy: Public
Dress code: Golf attire
Golf fees:
Weekdays $35
Weekends $40
Cart fees: $20
Carts on cart path only: No
Caddies: No
Guests carry bags: Yes
Guests pull carts: Yes
Golf packages: No

Location: Hwy.1 to Torrey Pines Rd. Just south of La Jolla.

Meadowood Resort
...continued from page 49
Meadowood is the headquarters for the prestigious Napa Valley Vintner's Association, and every June a three-day wine auction is held there. Although there aren't any grapevines on the property, the wine connection is one inevitably bred of location and clientele.

The Inn at Spanish Bay
...continued from page 57
There are eight championship tennis courts, including two night-lighted, and a stadium court designed for tournaments.

Horseback riding can be arranged by the respected Pebble Beach Equestrian Center.

The Lodge at Pebble Beach
...continued from page 59
Oh yes. Why doesn't the guy at the sandwich shop on the 9th tell us that, just 100 yards away, the sea gulls are waiting for our sandwich... He doesn't... so guess who goes without lunch! I can't prove it, but I'll bet that same guy is back there laughing behind his ketchup and mustard. Someday the "Golf-Fairy" will get even with him....

Hyatt Grand Champions
...continued from page 81
After a hard day of golf or tennis, one can relax around one of the four luxuriously landscaped pools or be pampered at the Spa with a massage, steam bath or sauna. The Swiss-inspired Health Club offers fitness equipment and aerobic classes.

And for the children... Camp Little Champions offers planned activities during the day, and lunch for children ages 3-5. For a fee, of course.

Silverado
...continued from page 55
Location: Hwy.80 to Sacramento. Take the #37 West exit (at Vallejo). Continue On #37 for 2 miles. Turn right on Hwy.29 North 2 miles to Napa. Follow all directional signs to Lake Berryessa. Turn left on Atlas Peak Rd.

The Inn at Spanish Bay
...continued from page 57
Location: Hwy.101 to the Monterey Penninsula turn-off, 156 west, to Hwy.1 south to the 17-Mile Dr./Pebble Beach exit. A guard at the entrance gate will direct you to the resort.

Industry Hills
...continued from page 83
Location: Fwy 60, exit Azusa Ave. then North to Industry Hills Parkway, or Fwy. 10, exit Azusa Ave. Then South to Industry Hills Parkway. Aprox 25 min. from Downtown Los Angeles.

La Quinta Hotel
...continued from page 87
Location: I-5 or Hwy 111 turn South on Washington Ave., then right on Eisenhower Ave.

Rancho Bernardo Inn

...continued from page 99

a massage room and fresh juice bar. Not to be overlooked is the 27-hole executive course rated as one of the finest in the country.

Eight red-tiled haciendas with their individual lobbies, contain 287 deluxe rooms or one-and-two-bedroom suites with their own private balconies.

Singing Hills Country Club and Resort

..continued from page 103

The restaurant is unpretentious, with friendly service and good, hearty food. The lounge has piano music and a small dance floor.

San Diego, only 18 miles away, has one of the most important zoos in the country, plus Sea World, both, a must for all ages.

Lawrence Welk Resort

..continued from page 89

Cart fees: ***Fountains:*** $20.
Meadow Lake: Incl.
Carts on cart path only:
Fountains: Yes
Meadow Lake: Yes w/ 90° rule
Caddies: No
Guests carry bags: No
Guests pull carts: No
Golf packages: Yes
Pro-shop phone:
Fountains:
(619)749-3225
Meadow Lake:
(619)749-1620
Location: Hwy.15 exit East on Gopher Canyon Rd. to Mountain Medow Rd. and left to Lawrence Welk Resort.

Ranchos Las Palmas

...continued from page 97

Pro-shop phone:
(619)568-2727
Location: Hwy.111 or I-10 to Bob Hope turn off.

Singing Hills Country Club

...continued from page 103

Location: I-8, exit on 2nd. offramp. 1.2 miles to Washington St., turn left to Granite Hills Rd. Go left, then an immediate right to Dehesa Rd. Approx. 2.2 miles to club entrance.

Trip Diary...

Trip Diary...

Trip Diary...

Trip Diary...

Trip Diary...

Trip Diary...

Are You Looking For a Gift For Your Favorite Golfer?

..........**GOLF VACATIONS IN CALIFORNIA**
A comprehensive book listing all golf resorts
in California $14.95

..........**GOLF VACATIONS IN ARIZONA**
A comprehensive book listing all golf resorts
in Arizona $14.95

..........**GOLF SCORE CARDS.** A gift for the avid golfer.
Original golf score cards from all golf resorts in
California and Arizona.
California $11.95
Arizona $11.95

...........**COLORFUL RESORT BROCHURES**
from the resorts listed in the books GOLF VACATIONS
IN CALIFORNIA and GOLF VACATIONS IN ARIZONA.
All inclusive rates and "golf packages". One call to us
and you'll get all the available marketing material from
each resort.
California $9.95
Arizona $9.95

All items relating to California are available for immediate shipment. The Arizona items will be available for shipment December 1, 1990.

To place your order with Pinehurst Publishing, Inc., please use the Order Form on the reverse side. FAX (213)545-8971 or call us at (213)545-3318.

Order Form

Qty.	Title/Item	Price	Total Price
____	California Golf Vacations	$14.95	________
____	Arizona Golf Vacations	$14.95	________
____	Golf Score Cards/California	$11.95	________
____	Golf Score Cards/Arizona	$11.95	________
____	Resort Brochures/California	$9.95	________
____	Resort Brochures/Arizona	$9.95	________
		Subtotal	________
		Shipping Expense for 1st Item:	$2.00
		For each additional item add 75¢	________
		For shipments in CA add 6.75% tax	________
		TOTAL price of items	________

[ ] Check enclosed with order payable to Pinehurst Publishing, Inc.
[ ] Please charge my credit card.
[ ]VISA [ ]Mastercard
Credit card #____________________________ Exp. date ____/____
Signature ______________________________

For quantity discounts, call (213)545-3318 or FAX (213)545-8971

SHIP TO:
Name:____
Address:____
City:___________________________State:________Zip____________

I understand that if I am not satisfied with any book or product, I may return the same for a full refund.

Pinehurst Publishing, Inc.
P. O. Box 3144-A
Manhattan Beach, CA 90266

Are You Looking For a Gift For Your Favorite Golfer?

..........**GOLF VACATIONS IN CALIFORNIA**
A comprehensive book listing all golf resorts in California $14.95

..........**GOLF VACATIONS IN ARIZONA**
A comprehensive book listing all golf resorts in Arizona $14.95

..........**GOLF SCORE CARDS.** A gift for the avid golfer. Original golf score cards from all golf resorts in California and Arizona.
California $11.95
Arizona $11.95

..........**COLORFUL RESORT BROCHURES**
from the resorts listed in the books GOLF VACATIONS IN CALIFORNIA and GOLF VACATIONS IN ARIZONA. All inclusive rates and "golf packages". One call to us and you'll get all the available marketing material from each resort.
California $9.95
Arizona $9.95

All items relating to California are available for immediate shipment. The Arizona items will be available for shipment December 1, 1990.

To place your order with Pinehurst Publishing, Inc., please use the Order Form on the reverse side. FAX (213)545-8971 or call us at (213)545-3318.

Order Form

Qty.	Title/Item	Price	Total Price
_____	California Golf Vacations	$14.95	_______
_____	Arizona Golf Vacations	$14.95	_______
_____	Golf Score Cards/California	$11.95	_______
_____	Golf Score Cards/Arizona	$11.95	_______
_____	Resort Brochures/California	$9.95	_______
_____	Resort Brochures/Arizona	$9.95	_______
		Subtotal	_______
		Shipping Expense for 1st Item:	$2.00
		For each additional item add 75¢	_______
		For shipments in CA add 6.75% tax	_______
		TOTAL price of items	_______

[ ] Check enclosed with order payable to Pinehurst Publishing, Inc.

For quantity discounts, call (213)545-3318 or FAX (213)545-8971

SHIP TO:

Name:____

Address:____

City:______________________________State:________Zip___________

I understand that if I am not satisfied with any book or product, I may return the same for a full refund.

Pinehurst Publishing, Inc.
P. O. Box 3144-A
Manhattan Beach, CA 90266